CORRECTION NOTICE TO READER

Builder's Book, Inc. and Xavier G.M. Zeitoun apologize for the inconvenience that may have resulted from the wrong typing and/or spelling of names, foreign or domestic, and company names as well as trademarks.

Subsequently, the following is to be read:

1. On all pages, the use of the name Pittsburgh Corning Corporation should read:
    Pittsburgh Corning Corporation or
    PC® or
    PC GlassBlock® Products

2. Page 24: the fax number for Pittsburgh Corning Corporation is: 412 / 327-5890.

3. Page 24: the patterns available are DECORA®, ARGUS®, VUE® (not "Clear"), ESSEX® AA, DELPHI®, CIRRUS®. Pattern no longer available are TEXTRA™ as well as solar block and metric block.

4. Page 19: a more correct description would be "...two by two to be *heat sealed*. The seal edges of the two halves are heated to a temperature of approximately 800ºC."

5. Page 70: read Pittsburgh Corning DECORA® pattern.

Thank you.

GLASS BLOCK HANDBOOK ©

by

XAVIER G.M. ZEITOUN

GLASS BLOCK HANDBOOK ©

by

XAVIER G.M. ZEITOUN

© COPYRIGHT 1995
by
XAVIER G.M. ZEITOUN AND BUILDER'S BOOK, INC.

**Published by
Builder's Book, Inc.
8001 Canoga Avenue
CANOGA PARK, CA 91304
818-887-7828
1-800-273-7375**

NOTICE TO READER : All rights reserved. This publication may not be duplicated in any way without the written consent of Builder's Book, Inc. and Xavier G.M. Zeitoun, except in the form of brief excerpts or quotations for the purpose of review. The information contained herein may not be duplicated, reproduced or transmitted in other books, databases or any other medium or any forms by any means, electronic, digital or mechanical, including photocopying, recording, or by any information storage and retrieval system without the written consent of Builder's Book, Inc. and Xavier G.M. Zeitoun. Making copy of this book, or any portion for any purpose other than for your personal use, is a violation of United States copyrights laws. All suggested practices, helpful hints and methods described are the sole responsibility of the reader.

Printed in the United States of America

Contents

Acknowledgements — *page 3*

Preface — *page 5*

1 - History — *page 6*

2 - Manufacturing — *page 17*

3 - Manufacturers — *page 23*

4 - Uses and Applications — *page 31*

5 - Advantages and Physical Properties — *page 36*

6 - Specifications and Standards Requirements — *page 51*

7 - Details and finishes — *page 82*

8 - Design and selection — *page 98*

9 - Installation — *page 116*

Bibliography — *page 176*

References and technical assistance — *page 177*

Glossary — *page 178*

Index — *page 180*

Acknowledgements and Thanks

I would like to extend my gratitude and thanks to the many people who have contributed their time, expertise, guidance, dedication and patience during the years that the quest for information has taken to result in the necessary fabric for the development of this book. It must be understood that some of these entities neither reviewed nor approved the content of this book prior to publication, but provided positions and informal interpretations on specific issues that were utilized to develop the information presented. While every effort has been made to accurately reflect the most reliable direction between differing jurisdictional authorities, it is the responsibility of the reader to verify correct interpretations of conflicting requirements that may arise between State and Federal sources. These entities cannot be held responsible for the Author's assessment of these situations.

Circle Redmont, Fred Saunder Jr. and Sr. and all of you out there, Sony, Virginia.
Pittsburgh-Corning, Bob DeGusipe, Barbara J.Lowrie
John Morehart, Glass Block Unlimited
Carl Lambert, an attorney in Santa Monica, California.
Richard Hoffman, attorney and friend of Los Angeles Bar Association.
Association des Amis de la Maison de Verre, in Paris, France.

I would like to extend special thanks to Oussa Awad, Builder's Book Inc., in Canoga Park, California for the constant support and assistance he has given me in the production of this book. Neva Jakich, who has assisted and encouraged me in the making of this project. My sister Nathalie who gathered information from Paris, France, as well as my mother and father; Terry Ilous and Jim Zarinfar; Karri and Joshua Cohen.

I dedicate this book to my son, Talun.

PREFACE

This manual endeavors to fill the void in information and access for a product that has seen a spectacular rise in use and interest over the last decade. This success pushes the Glass Block into a category of its own, although more often than not it is wrongfully lumped in with masonry, glazing or tile.

My intent is to provide practical information for all those who have a need for using Glass Block, such as architects, designers, engineers and contractors. It also aim at answering the many questions I have been asked over the years from homeowners, suppliers and installers.

References of measure will be in the American Standard system, with the international metric system also indicated. All brands of Glass Blocks now offers both systems' sizing. Throughout the manual I use manufacturers specifications most commonly used in the present international market. A chapter contains manufacturers' locations and the appropriate contact therein.

Chapter 1

History

Naturally, glass block is a product of glass. A complete history of the discovery and manufacture of glass making is not the purpose of this manual but we should like to pay a small tribute to one of the oldest manufactured products that has evolved to become an art form through the course of history.

The story would start five thousand years ago in Mesopotamia (modern Iraq) with the appearance of glass casting (versus glass blowing) which was used in the earliest production of glass blocks around 1500 A.D in Egypt, and quickly spread through the Roman Empire to Asia and the Orient.

The effect of history and culture in Europe (and later in America), sees the glass block being developed particularly in French and German architecture, before the first world war. Originally, glass blocks were made by hand, compressing together fewer sections of standard glass, usually cut into small sizes. Their use was purely functional in "utility" type of buildings. It could be said they are the ancestor of the modern skylight.

As early as 1809, it has been reported that glass illuminators were used to "admit daylight into the internal parts of ships and buildings". An early example of its use is in the St Paul's Churchyard in London. In the early 1800's, "cellular lights", as they were called, were described as "thick circular slabs in stone or bedded in an iron frame". Metal framed pavement lights appeared in France and Germany as early as 1907.

In the second half of the 19th century, mouth blown and circular sections of glass were used in single units in unimportant rooms designated for cellars or similar spaces and did not attract much attention. However, developments in related industries changed its status. The invention of reinforced concrete, used by Monier in 1897, paved the way for glass block units to be supported within larger surfaces. The Lubber machine, invented in 1903, was the first glass manufacturing machine allowed to be used in construction resulting in the first dome, made of concrete and glass by Joachim, a French architect.

In 1907, Friedich Keppler patented a solid glass block of four to six and-a-half centimeters in thickness (approximately one and a half to two and a half inches). In France in 1908, the above mentioned Joachim applied for the patent "Le beton arme translucide" (the translucent reinforced concrete) or reinforced glass concrete, where structural stress is transmitted to glass when combined with metal and/or concrete.

In Germany, gigantic machines were in use made by Siemens and Luxer-Prismen-Gesseschaft. In France, Albert Gerrer developed the Falconier process, which was the first to assemble the two halves of mouth-blown glass block, sealed at temperature while cooling down from forming - the basis which still applies today. Toughened lenses were developed in the early 1930's by Saint Gobain Glass Company in France and glass walls were introduced.

In the United States, one of the first applications was done in 1910, when glass and concrete roof lights were used in the Kodak Building. It was during the recession of 1929 that Owens-Illinois and Corning-Reubens, giants of American industry, developed and produced the hollow glass blocks, with fewer sizes and patterns. In 1935, Corning Glass Works developed the Corning-Steuben block manufactured with heat resistant glass and partially evacuated during production. This was the forerunner to Pittsburgh Corning's original product. It was further developed at the Company's plant in Charleroi, Pennsylvania.

Creative architects coupled with new schools of thought facilitated a rapid development put America in the forefront of the movement. Glass block became a symbol for Art Deco and was one of the most featured items of interior design and construction in Modern, Contemporary and Post-Modern architecture in the United States, Europe and Japan.

La Maison De Verre, Paris, France.

La Maison De Verre, Paris, France.

This burgeoning commercialization continued until the early thirties, but did not endure the second World War. There was a sudden decline and loss of interest until the late sixties when a resurgence of glass block usage occurred, and still continues to gain popularity and respect. After the War, machinery and technology improves and more attention was paid to the architectural qualities of glass blocks. Architectural schools of thought such as Le Corbusier in France and Otto Haesler in Germany really supported their use and gave the product the potential for expansion. "La Maison de Verre" (the House of Glass), shown on following page, was designed by Pierre Charreau and Bernard Bijvoet, and was built in Paris, between 1928 and 1932. It still stands in pristine condition through the years. This spectacular edifice is the result of a total remodeling of an 18th century hotel building. At the time, it raised shock and astonishment from popular Press both in France and abroad. It was the true start of the first residential application for glass block.

Other applications quickly followed. Theaters and other large public facilities which are still in perfect condition and maintain their impact, owe their beauty to the use of glass block. More and more, this revived invention is universally praised for its excellent physical properties, multiple advantages and versatility of use. Currently in the United States and other countries, it is a thriving industry, boosted by the universal need for its correlation of advantages - secure, durable, low maintenance and particular elegance and beauty.

In the early thirties, Pittsburgh-Corning® was a consumer oriented company with little knowledge of the building and construction market. They approached the Pittsburgh Plate Glass Company with the idea of a joint venture to further develop and promote this new building product. The Pittsburgh-Corning Corporation® was born.

Construction of the first plant began at Port Allegany, Pennsylvania in 1937, the same year the Pittsburgh-Corning Corporation® was chartered in the state of Pennsylvania. The Pittsburgh-Corning® glass block units first came off the production line at Plant 1 on February 8, 1938 in Decora® and Argus® patterns. These patterns are still very popular selections fifty years later in today's market.

When the sales of glass block declined in the late seventies, Pittsburgh-Corning®, the sole manufacturer of glass block in the U.S, announced its intent to discontinue making the products manufactured since 1937. Following an announcement by the editor of **Progressive Architecture**, a major architectural publication in the United States, that the U.S manufactured glass block products were soon to be unavailable, letters poured in to the management at Pittsburgh-Corning Corporation® from principals of prominent architectural firms. Affirming their interest in the products and assuring Pittsburgh-Corning® they had already specified Pittsburgh-Corning® glass block units for numerous design projects soon to be underway. They asked that Pittsburgh-Corning® seriously reconsider their decision to terminate the manufacture of its glass block products. In response, Pittsburgh-Corning® not only reversed its decision, but launched a major update of their production facilities to meet the resurgent demand for its product. Continuing popularity and a steadily increasing demand for their glass block units in the 1980's resulted in two major plant modernizations at its Port Allegany, Pennsylvania facility within five years.

Today, the Pittsburgh-Corning® Company remains committed to meeting the ever growing demand for their glass block products in the many market places it serves worldwide.

Plaza Center
Architect: Luigi Bianco, ASID, IBD
Photographer: Robert Perron
Pittsburgh Corning Products
Vue® Pattern & Hedron® Corner Block
(Solar Reflective Coating)

Chapter 2

Manufacturing

As previously mentioned, glass block owes its composition and basic ingredients to glass commonly used in window, plate or float application. Because of its extreme versatility, glass, when at fusion level, can be formed, blown, pressed, pulled, molded or cast as needed. When cooled and stabilized, it can be cut, engraved, stained or painted. Glass block is a form of the technique of mold casting, giving it limitless possibilities in terms of creation and design.

The basic raw ingredients of glass are very carefully selected. Three main components are needed:

1. **Silica sand** (SiO_2) is the primary substance with an approximate and variable amount of 50-60%. The sand must be exceptionally pure and with a low iron content.
2. **Oxide of Sodium** (Na_2O), a secondary substance, amounts approximately 10-15%. Also called *Soda*.
3. **Calcium Oxide** (Ca_2O) or *Lime*. Approximately 8-10%. Oxides of Boron, Magnesium, Aluminum and Potassium as well as other crystalline items that may be carbonates and nitrates and various additives. Sometimes scrap glass may be added to ameliorate the process.

These raw materials are then crushed, powdered, filtered and purified in a mechanical process to be uniformly distributed and "electron-organized". The mixture is then batched into crucibles to be put in furnaces and heated. Melting will occur at a temperature of 1400-1500 °C (centigrade Celsius - approximately 2550-2730 °F or Fahrenheit). It now has a viscous texture, like melted Swiss cheese. The vitreous mass is maintained for refining at a high temperature and then dropped to about 1200 °C (2190 °F) for de-gasseifying and down to 1100 °C (2010 °F) so it can be formed.

A small amount of this molten glass obtained is dripped into a female mold, piston type; this plunger forces the molten liquid glass to fill each details of the female one as well as the male, which has a different surface design at the bottom to create the appropriate final glass block design. This process generates the halves of glass blocks.

Glass block assembling
Courtesy of Pittsburgh-Corning ©

In the second step of the process, those dish-shaped units, identical in size and pattern are picked up and selected two by two to be "forge-welded". The perimeter edges of the two halves are reheated at a temperature of approximately 800 ºC

(1470 ºF), and then fused together by slight pressure, about 1.3 atm. During this fusion, a partial vacuum (nearly 70%) is completed in the cavity creating a below normal air pressure. It is interesting to note that this feature explains the startling "popping" explosion noise heard when a glass block fractures. It is too that chamber that confers to the hollow unit most of its astonishing properties and performances as a heat and sound insulator, added to the one of glass itself.

All lateral edges of the glass block are then corrugated and treated with a moisture resistant bonding agent and metal oxide type coating material. Its appearance varies according to each manufacturer. Usually, a white primer is added to most of imported glass blocks, while the American counterpart is using a translucent type. That edge coating also gives a good bonding surface and allows adhesion to the mortar. It also prevent any mortar voids that can occur during vertical mortar installations; these voids could be easily seen through the side of the more translucent patterns of glass blocks.

Let's note here that this same characteristic of influence from the edges is utilized to give a color accent to the panel installed, by either using a colored coat edge or by adding color to the mortar, as for regular concrete coloring. This colored edge coating or colored mortar will tend to affect the whole tone of the wall. The coloring technique described above is widely used by all the manufacturers.

There are actually two popular types of glass blocks manufactured. The most popular is the hollow unit, whose fabrication is described earlier in this chapter, and the other is a one half unit, commonly called paver, mostly used for structural metal or concrete inserts into a wide range of applications reaching from skylight to floor tile. Another variation to these two types is a solid glass block unit, usually offered by manufacturers into a one size one pattern unit, because of its difficulty to be perfectly produced. It is usually three inches thick (90 millimeters) and has been proven in tests to be virtually bullet proof.

The long list of patterns and sizes generated by this manufacturing process will be detailed in a later section of this manual. However, they are generally limited to a minimum size of about four inches to a maximum presently marketed of 12 inches (10 to 30 centimeters), round or square. The thickness of hollow units are represented by two sizes commonly used in the metric system and American standard - three inches (90 millimeters) and four inches (120 millimeters). For accurate and exact sizes, see chapter 6.

Glass block manufacturing
Courtesy of Pittsburgh-Corning ©

Chapter 3

Manufacturers

In the quest for the most suitable brand of glass block for your particular need, the increasing public demand may make you feel you are chasing the seller. If you find a lack of access and information, it may be due to fierce competition and "territorial" rights among suppliers. The good old "yellow pages" will unearth local suppliers. The large building material discount establishments usually have poor quantities available and a restricted choice of patterns and sizes.

The search for the right manufacturer is also narrowed because of the small number of manufacturers existing or the political monopoly of the existing ones. I think this applies to any territorial marketing maneuver in the world. Often, local and federal testing requirements for glass blocks (understandable if quality is to be maintained) cause delays and advertising deficiencies.

Hopefully, the following manufacturers' information will assist you, and narrow down any possible problems you may encounter in the marriage of supply and demand.

PITTSBURGH-CORNING® U.S.A

Pittsburgh-Corning Corporation
800 Presque Isle Drive
Pittsburgh, Pennsylvania 15239
Tel.:412-327-6100
Telex:44-23018
Fax:412-733-4815

The most distributed manufacturer, throughout in the U.S.A, with several different patterns available (Decora, Argus, Clear, Essex AA, Delphi, Tetra, Cirrus). Standard American, Metric available. Carries most common sizes. Good list of miscellaneous such as end blocks, corners, 45 angle, fire rated blocks, solar, edge coated and solid glass blocks. Complete line of accessories and sub materials for installation, applications and enhancement. Has all technical and information support for trade and public. Also Hot Line available: 800-992-5769.

SOLARIS® GERMANY

WESTERWALD AG
WESTER, WALDAG, WIRGES
Postfach, 1120
5432 Wirges
Tel.:49-2602-681275
Fax:49-2602-681416
Telex:869662 WWGL

Classified in 08810/SOA, Buy Line 2550. Widely distributed in Europe and U.S.A. Limited patterns and sizes available. Colored blocks. Corner and end blocks limited, no fire rated blocks. Metric and standard sizes.

WECK® GERMANY

Distributed by:
Glashaus Inc.
415 West Golf Road
Suite 13
Arlinton-Heights, Illinois
Tel.:708-640-6910
Fax:708-640-6955

One of the first manufacturer in Europe and importers into the U.S.A. Very competitive to its American competitor. Carries most popular patterns but with a different name to its American equivalent: Nubio (equivalent to Decora), X-ribbed (equivalent to Argus), Clarity (equivalent to Clear), Spray (equivalent to Essex AA), Aktis (equivalent to Delphi). Has available a wide variety of exotic design and patterns in its standard and metric line. Corners, end blocks, solar, fire rated blocks and colored blocks.

IPERFAN®　　　　　　　　　　　　　　　　　　**ITALY**

Vettromatone

FIDENZIA VETRARIA INDUSTRIALE

Vialla Martiri della Liberta, I

Fidenza, Italy PR 43036

Tel.:0524-511-1

Telex:531371 Fidret I

Fax:0524-84908

FIDENZA VETRARIA SPA

Via Felice Casati, 32

20124 Milano, TO

Tel.:02-6260

Telex:330866 Fidvet

Characterized by its crystal and colorless glass. Mainly metric sizes, fewer standard sizes. Not competitive in market. All sizes and patterns, with a myriad range of design patterns. Accessories and cladding system available. U.S representative:

Don Flanders

3911 S.Mariposa St.

Englewood, CO 80110

Tel.:303-762-9330

GERRIX-GLASSTEINE®　　　　　　　　　　**GERMANY**

GERRESHEIMER

GLAS AKTIENGESELLSCHAFT

Verkauf Bauglas

Postfach 120210

Heyestrabe 178

D.4000 Dusseldorf 12

Tel.:02111-28-09-9

Telex:8-587-561 GXBD

American and European Standards, large variety of patterns. all sizes. Variety of bronze colored glass blocks.

SAINT GOBAIN® FRANCE

Also includes Vegla line.

EXPORT COORDINATION CENTER
EXPROVER S.A
Avenue de Tervuren, Bte 4
B-1150 Brussels, Belgium
Tel.:32-2-762-8242
Fax:32-2-762-8761

Represented in U.S.A and Canada by:

EUROGLASS GLASREP CORPORATION
123 Main Street, Suite 920
White Plains, NY 10601
Tel.:914-683-1390
Fax:914-683-6704
Telex:420 474

All sizes and patterns available. Metric and standard, hollow and slid glass blocks, colored glass. St Gobain recently acquired Solaris in January 1992.

N.E.G® JAPAN

Nippon Electric Glass Co., Ltd
Building Material Division
1-4, Mihyara 4-chome, Yodogawa-ku
Osaka 532, Japan
Phone: 06-399-2721
Telex: 523-3885 NEGLAS J
Cable: NEGLASS OSAKA
FAX: 06-399-2731

All sizes and patterns, American Standards and Metric System.

The **IDG** Glass Block information service: the IDG is the joint service of the German glass block manufacturers. The purpose of the IDG is to promote Glass Block architecture and show the exemplary use of Glass Blocks. The IDG is responsible for public relation work on up to date application of Glass Block architecture.

The IDG also regards itself as a collector of ideas and historical traditions and the further conceptional development of the idea of the interaction between light and space as the central concept in the use of glass block architecture.

The IDG includes WECK®, SOLARIS® (recently acquired by St. Gobain), VEGLA® and GERRIX®.

Pittsburgh Corning Glass Block® FAMILY PHOTO

Chapter 4

Uses and Applications

Today's modern architecture and style evolution promotes and calls for new "high tech" product and intense reevaluation of all kinds of materials. Glass block is part and parcel of these changes. It is a unique item that combines good taste with need, contains many advantages while providing interest to the purveyor. Its physical properties are a great attribute along with the aesthetic value. Glass block is all at once, functional and expressive, delicate and radiant, and delivers dramatic strength and beauty.

At the architect/designer level or homeowner/contractor stage, I have often seen glass block application resolve problem situations in the course of new construction or remodeling. During the lengthy discussions that precede a unanimous decision among the persons involved in a building project, I have seen all types of people, taste and culture notwithstanding, hesitate at first but ultimately amazed and thankful at the simple beauty of a finished glass block wall.

Despite the prolonged absence of use and the resulting decline mentioned earlier, the prevalence of glass block in any city anywhere in the world, from a single insert of a glass masonry unit inside a residential home to entire walls in building, it still maintains an impact, and was bound to re emerge. Following are some suggested uses in the endless list of possibilities provided by glass block construction. These are the most commonly preferred locations picked either in a family residence or in a commercial project.

In residential...

Interior panels and dividers, full height or counter height. Panels of glass block will keep a surprising strength while only attached at its base and free standing on one, two or three sides.

Stairwells, long, vertical or horizontal one block wide strips, stepped curved stairwell window openings are very popular, being an area where light is imperative without necessary ventilation. Structural steel applications will allow it to go several stories high (see Chapter 6: Specifications, about size limits and Chapter 9: Installation) and can actually be an entire elevator shaft.

Free standing walls may be very large but could require additional anchors embedded into floor structure (slab or other)

All kinds of windows, especially in bathrooms and kitchens, with hundreds of possible designs by mixing sizes and patterns with your imagination as described in Chapter 8: Design and Selection.

Shower walls, partial or total enclosure is one of the primary residential demands. They are fully up to construction standards. Glass block installed in mortar is excellent for water-tight specifications. So you can assure the homeowner that "it won't leak!", assuming good workmanship, which is crucial to glass block for results. Corner blocks and end blocks have various patterns and sizes which make use in the shower or steam room ideal. Moreover, the shower door can have its light gauge aluminum frame screwed or bolted permanently and securely between the glass blocks at grout lines, using 1/4" plastic or metal anchors carefully fitted along with the appropriate screws.

Bars and counters for reception areas are also a growing trend. As mentioned above, free standing curved or cornered low wall of mortared glass block panels, is extremely strong and durable. These types of walls will easily support any complementing material (wood, glass, marble, granite etc...) and no matter who wishes to dance on the surface while in a party mood should be able to see the night out! An added feature in this type of installation can be electric light. A small neon fixture or fiber optic can make an interesting dramatic effect (see Chapter 9: Installations procedures).

Everyone has possibly walked through a door entrance with glass block side lights, at one or both sides of a French door or any solid wooden door. It adds light in entrances and also puts out a strong security appearance. Low maintenance is appreciated in this application and more about maintenance is in the next chapter.

Skylights, stair railings (banisters), accented flooring, columns for a driveway entrance, or a standout mailbox, let your imagination find the rest.

In commercial...

Because of the versatility of glass block in combining light requirements, low cost maintenance, visibility and security, architects will often "spec" glass block for cultural, sports, commercial and recreational facilities.

Schools and hospitals, medical offices are frequent and heavy users of glass blocks. It gives these types of area an eye catching and relaxing feeling which by their very nature are sometimes not the most attractive place people want to visit. The pristine effect that can be created is perfect for these particular places of business.

Sporting centers and gymnasiums are ideal for glass blocks.

Warehouses, factories and the such, appreciate the aspect of security where vandalism is a growing problem. Glass block will positively replace the combination frame windows and metal bars. Ventilation when required or necessary will be provided by vents and glass block accessories, that will be described in a following chapter.

Chapter 5

Advantages and Physical Properties

What makes glass block so popular and attractive? It seems the combination of beauty and sturdiness has allowed it to forge an enviable reputation in the building materials industry. Physical tests performed on the product, as specified by local and international construction requirements indicates a long list of advantages and good reason to adopt it for new construction. As in remodeling older structures, I have seen situations and locations where, for example, owner or designer seem to hesitate in selecting fix glass or window. When light is necessary but security a dominant concern, glass block always become the adequate material and solution.

This following list of beneficial characteristics should be evident in all glass block no matter whom the original manufacturer may be. Product development has been intense. Professional installation must be careful and precise and may very well affect the following:

1. Energy transmission, winter or summer.
2. Light transmission, as a glazing component.
3. Sound transmission, hollow or solid units.
4. Esthetic guaranty through proper workmanship.
5. Privacy potential regulator.
6. Moisture resistant and durable.
7. Low maintenance in cost and time.

1. **Energy transmission**

Coefficient heat transmission is 0.44 - 0.66, depending on manufacturer, pattern and size. As described in the manufacturing chapter, the two halves (or sections) of glass are pressed, fused and welded, creating a partial vacuum process, an air sealed and absolute tight chamber, No interior condensation is the amazing direct result of this process, even used under water as in a swimming pool, spa or a steam shower enclosure.

This advantage far outweighs the use of regular glass, because of its superior insulation qualities, it is ideally suited to air controlled buildings. In other words, it will self adapt to summer and winter climatic conditions. Glass block is often specified by architects and designers in cities or suburbs near the water area where a high level of efficiency for glazed area is required. These areas with a strong degree of humidity that is constantly a source of discomfort as well as inconvenience to inhabitants, are especially detrimental to numerous building materials. Not glass block! It laughs at salt and other eroding factors. The insulation value of a glass block is similar to 10 to 12 inches of solid concrete making it a wonderful solution to energy transmission problems.

D.1: Regular hollow glass block

Sunlight in summer

Sunlight in winter

Comparing glass to other glazing materials, the table D.1a compares heat transmission coefficient (U) and resistance (R) of glass, plastic and glass blocks.

2. Light transmission

Light transmission is approximately 50-85%, it also varies according to type and pattern and is probably the most important factor for architects and homeowners. Glass block keeps all the quality of glass while controlling and regulating the flow of

D.1a: Thermal resistance of Glazing materials

MATERIALS	HEAT TRANSMISSION COEFFICIENT (U)	SEASONS	RESISTANCE (R)
Exterior vertical panels			
Flat glass, Single glass	1.10	Winter	0.91
	1.04	Summer	0.96
Insulating glass, two layers			
with 3/16" airspace	0.62	Winter	1.61
	0.65	Summer	1.54
with 1/4" airspace	0.56	Winter	1.72
	0.61	Summer	1.64
with 1/2" airspace	0.49	Winter	2.04
	0.56	Summer	1.79
Insulating glass, three layers			
with 1/4" airspace	0.39	Winter	2.56
	0.44	Summer	2.22
with 1/2" airspace	0.31	Winter	3.23
	0.39	Summer	2.56
with 1/2" airspace, low remittance coating			
e=20	0.32	Winter	3.13
	0.38	Summer	2.63
e=40	0.38	Winter	2.63
	0.45	Summer	2.22
e=60	0.43	Winter	2.33
	0.51	Summer	1.96
Storm windows			
1-4" airspace	0.50	Winter	2.00
	0.50	Summer	2.00
Glass Block			
6 x 6 x 4 (nominal)	**0.60**	**Winter**	**1.67**
	0.57	**Summer**	**1.76**
8 x 8 x 4 (nominal)	**0.56**	**Winter**	**1.79**
	0.54	**Summer**	**1.85**
with fibrous insert	**0.48**	**Winter**	**2.06**
	0.46	**Summer**	**2.17**
12 x 12 x 4 (nominal)	**0.52**	**Winter**	**1.92**
	0.50	**Summer**	**2.00**
with fibrous insert	**0.44**	**Winter**	**2.27**
	0.42	**Summer**	**2.38**
Single plastic sheet			
1/8" nominal thickness	1.06	Winter	0.94
	0.98	Summer	1.02
1/4" nominal thickness	0.96	Winter	1.04
	0.89	Summer	1.12
Exterior horizontal panels			
Flat glass, Single glass	1.23	Winter	0.81
	0.83	Summer	1.20
Insulating glass, two layers			
with 3/16" airspace	0.70	Winter	1.43
	0.57	Summer	1.75
with 1/4" airspace	0.65	Winter	1.54
	0.54	Summer	1.85
with 1/2" airspace	0.59	Winter	1.69
	0.49	Summer	2.04
Glass Block			
12 x 12 x 4 (nominal)			
with fibrous insert	**0.51**	**Winter**	**1.96**
	0.34	**Summer**	**2.94**

light in terms of diffusion, refraction, convection and distribution. Building orientation and sun exposure will determine location of a panel (with respect to local building codes). Then the desired intensity of illumination and effect needed for the room according to its size and function, should lead to the final decision for the size and pattern to be used.

Light transmission will vary from 10 to 90%, depending upon patterns and manufacturers (see tables in the following chapter for references).

Where brightness is a requirement and privacy an issue, I would suggest Decora, (or Cloud, Nubio - depending upon the manufacturer) . Clear or Vue, is basically a non patterned glass block, used where visibility is solicited. Ripple, Argus or X-Ribbed, which is a striped design, will redirect light and also give great privacy. This is the oldest and one of the first pattern manufactured; vertical lines on one side and horizontal on the other side will give a squared effect when submitted through natural or artificial light.

Of course, these patterns will also affect the privacy factor. Some patterns are especially made to deal with light accents such as light directive unit. For example, the Essex AA from Pittsburgh-Corning or the "light directive" from N.E.G, which, similarly to the ripple, offers a quantity of lines opposite in direction from both sides, and will provide the desired effect, in terms of light filtration and orientation.

Where minimal brightness is required, or high sun exposure prevails, solar reflective glass block is available. An oxide coating is applied to one face of the block and will affect light and heat transmission. It results in an impressive visual effect from the exterior and adds to the aesthetic enjoyment from inside. The Company offers an interesting variation: the "LX series", made for both light and privacy purposes. A white, thin fibrous membrane is inserted between both sections of a hollow block at time of fusion of both halves, keeping the glass pattern and design effective, reducing the diffusion of bright light and totally "blocking" the sight.

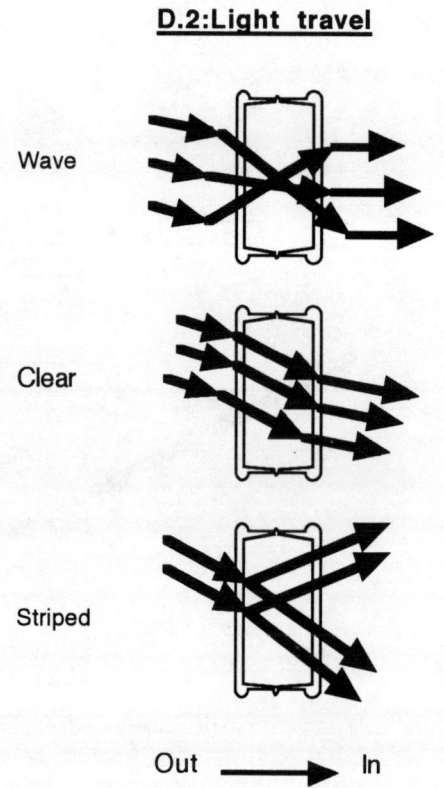

D.2:Light travel

D.3: Regular hollow glass block light transmission

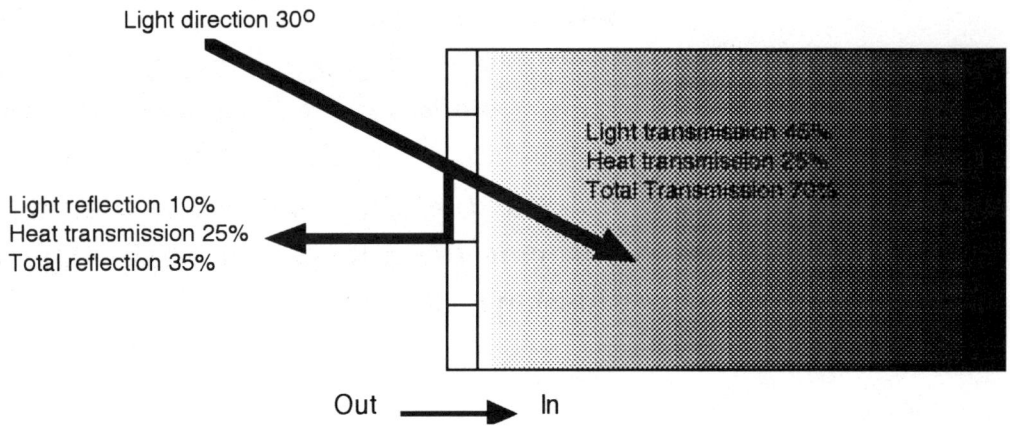

D.4: Solar reflective glass block light transmission

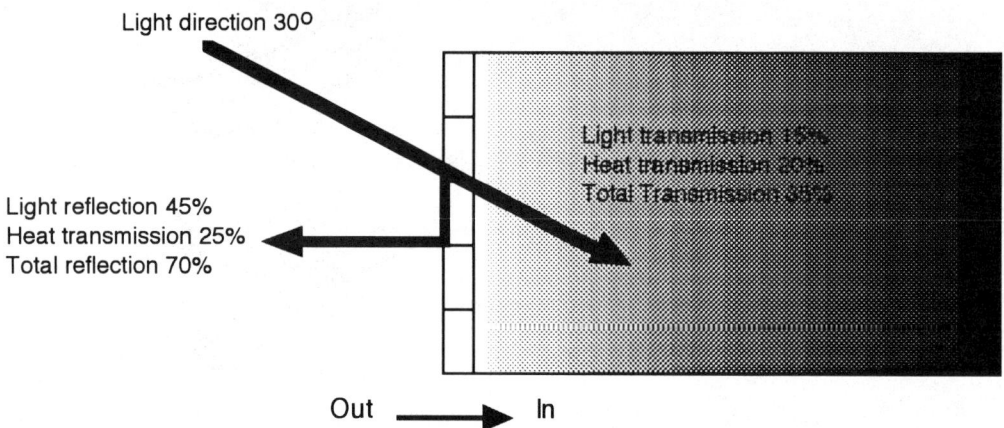

Another alternative is to sandblast one or both sides of the unit, usually with sand or metal or a mix of metal and glass debris, giving several grades and appearances to the process. This added cost can be justified as it creates such a special "look".

3. Sound transmission

An approximate reduction of under 37 decibels is achieved with glass block.

The sealed chamber of evacuated air produced at fusion temperature makes glass block an excellent sound retardant. Connected with its proper mortar joints, installed glass block panels will ensure a sound transmission loss (average decibel loss of sound passing through the wall) ranging from 37 to 45 decibels (or Sound Transmission Class S.T.C- similar), here again depending on size and manufacturer.

D.6: Sound transmission chart

Transmission loss Db	29	29.5	31	37	39	42	45
Frequency Hz	125	175	250	350	500	700	1000

For instance, the use of glass block will render heavy freeway traffic to the value of domestic mumble (measuring 80 decibels); a noisy street will sound like a quiet office space (measuring 50 decibels). So, glass block is a positive choice for buildings in commercial and busy areas, near freeways or even airports.

4. High security glazing

Compressive strength resumes 400-850 lbf/in² or P.S.I of gross bearing area, again depending upon models and manufacturers. Although glass block is not structural and thus non load bearing, as specified in building codes, it is a positive factor to aid the stability of the structure. Add the compressive strength of type O or type N mortar required to its installation to its necessary reinforcement. That includes metal anchor, bolted or welded to structural members or channel, and horizontal 9 gauge double tie bar running between masonry unit courses. The whole combination is virtually vandal-proof. Forcible entry is unlikely, hazardous and useless. A direct hit in order to intentionally break a hollow unit, will discourage burglars as a mini type explosion will occur due to the release of the interior vacuum sealed air.

Also, glass block will resist high winds and threatening meteorological conditions (20 lbs/ft² or 47.88 N.m² or 2.753 to 4.137 MN/m²). Excellent fire rating tests (see fire rating) are shown further. It will stand shocks, impacts, moderate collisions and earthquakes.

Obviously, regular glass does not compare. Shattered panels are a rare occurrence when proportionally compared to standard glass. If there is a need to replace one glass block unit, it is possible and certainly less costly than replacing a good sized tempered front window unit. Some manufacturers offer a 60 minute and 90 minute fire rated block. There is also a solid block, about 3 inches thick and tested to be bullet proof and widely used in police and correctional facilities.

5. Aesthetic

Glass block fits most architecture styles and flatters all kinds of usages. It really can be installed anywhere and be appreciated. All at once, there is visual and tactile pleasure with a conversation piece attracting comment and interest, just like watching television or facing a soothing fire burning in the heart of a fireplace.

Workmanship is paramount for functional beauty. The versatility and flexibility of the product allows you numerous applications. It is an elegant and featured material, found in luxury buildings but also in common warehouses. The recent controversy about the high cost of glass block, in material and installation, seems to me ambiguous at most. The growing competition between manufacturers, suppliers and installers is making it more and more available and affordable right now.

Obviously the increasing demand is leveling the cost factor gradually. If I may stick my neck out regarding cost for a moment. For example, to build a shower wall enclosure, the cost of framing, insulation, wall covering, drywall or float, primer and paint, tiles or marble, will compare favorably to the cost of glass blocks. In fact, in many cases, the glass block cost will be very close in cost of time and labor, if not more less. Or, for that matter, let's take the example of an expensive window: probably dual glazing, tempered, mill, finishes, paint eventually louvers and security bars will still be as costly or more than its equivalent in glass blocks, labor and material, with a better result and appearance.

6. Privacy

The compromise between privacy and limited visual access is subject to great concern and different opinions. The sense of mystery gives glass block an added attraction. From the uninterrupted view given by a translucent pattern, made by all manufacturers, to a thin film of fiberglass that brings a curtain to a scene, the amount of patterns available from manufacturers will not fall to give a satisfactory choice in the degree of privacy.

We must note here that the mixed sense of prestige and mystery make glass block walls fascinating and exotic. Looking at a sight or trying to imagine it when facing a panel, or actually looking at it, has, we could say without drifting into extremes, a very relaxing power. Working or living around it, can be a little bit like a visit to an art exhibition. This feature, added to an aura of luxury, gives the product its own personalized definition of privacy. In my time as an installer, an incredible number of women voiced their concern with the inevitable question regarding the privacy provided by a glass block wall. As use in the bathroom is very common. It is a most legitimate query. Fears range from an indiscreet gardener or neighbor to a guest in the home. The solution is mainly in the choice of pattern (see graph) and assurances can be given depending on the distance between the outside of the glass wall and the viewpoint or scenery in a particular given area.

Glass block is not a visual barrier but a **limit to visual access**. Here is what you should know about a medium dense pattern, which is the most used on the market today:

* you can see forms, color and movements, or at least guess them
* the further you stand from the glass block, the most distorted the vision.
* from the exterior, natural light will act as a counter light, reducing the visibility.
* at night, inside light will then accentuate exposure.

Each situation is different of course, and discussion with an appropriate distributor or experienced installer will be helpful, and a solution can always be found, with the growing variety of block that is now available.

7. Moisture resistant

The moisture resistant property of the glass block inherent in its glass is the perfect example of non corrosive durability. The special mortar mix used, with its strength and density, enhances the block and makes it ideal for a shower, exterior window or skylight and ensures that its replacement may never be necessary. Good workmanship can ensure almost permanent usage.

None of the properties of glass block and its sub materials used for installation will rust, rot or corrode. All accessories, if properly handled, will resist the elements. Reinforcements and attachments are available in galvanized metal. The expansion material is polyethurane foam. Waterproofing admix recently developed by the construction industry can be easily added to the mortar composition for strength and as a water repellent.

8. Maintenance

Not only is glass block classy, strong, waterproof and secure, while giving the space light and also sound and heat insulation, it almost takes care of itself. What a welcome bonus for an attractive product - low cost, simple maintenance. It is almost dust proof (with the exception of exterior sides, especially in skylights and deck application. When needed (and that is seldom) use a damp cloth to wipe. Commercial products like windex or ammonia based sprays may be used without harm on the interior. For the outside wall, just water rinse with a hose on full pressure.

For easy cleaning traces of mortar, paint and plaster debris during and after installation, just use a fine steel wool that will not scratch the glass block.

Silicone installation (see chapter 9) requires more care and maintenance due to silicone and caulking materials tendency to attract and store dust as well as peeling, fading, discoloring and deteriorating over the years.

Appalachian State University, College of Business
Architect: J.N Pease Associates
Photographer: Gordon Schenck
Pittsburgh-Corning VUE® Pattern

Chapter 6

Specifications and Standard Requirements

This chapter will be of more interest to architects and designers as it refers to technical applications of glass block as a building material component and how specifications differ from each manufacturer. Contractors, suppliers and installers will find here the information useful regarding the main sub materials required through the various situations in the field.

Although glass block usage is enjoying a resurgence, there seems to be a disproportionate availability of informative literature. This could be because there is a debate whether the glass brick is a Masonry, Tile or Glazing component. It certainly can be purchased at large building material establishment as they have recently started stocking glass blocks, but variety is limited. The same could be said for a masonry supplier or tile specialist.

According to the State Contractor License Board and the related building codes throughout America, it is a C 29 masonry license that is required for glass block installation. The Standard Specification Institute circulates in section 04270 that it is a Glass Masonry Unit and clear fully distinct from Masonry 04000. I think it is important to keep the above in mind and if attention is paid to ensure its proper installation, the aesthetic and technical facets will be maintained.

This chapter contains two separate issues:

1. Legal aspect of the Building Code, including Californian Building Code and an approach from the American Institute of Architects.

2. General information and data from the main manufacturers, tests and reports.

1. Uniform Building Code
1991 edition and 1992 revisions.
Part V - Engineering regulations - Quality and Design of the Materials of Construction

CHAPTER 24 - MASONRY

General
Sec. 2401

(b) Definitions. Masonry Unit is brick, tile, stone, glass block or concrete block conforming to the requirements specified in section 2402.

Hollow unit masonry is a masonry unit whose cross sectional area in every plane parallel to the bearing surface is less than 75% of the cross sectional area in the same plane. Solid unit is more than 75%.

Material Standard
Sec. 2402

(b) Standards of quality. The standards listed below labeled a "U.B.C Standard" are also listed in Chapter 60, Part II, and are part of this code. The other standards listed below are guideline standards and as such are not adopted as part of this code (see sections 6002 and 6003).

6. Masonry Units. Other.

B. Glass Block.

(i) Glass block may be solid or hollow and contains inserts.

(ii) All mortar contact surfaces shall be treated to ensure adhesion between mortar and glass.

Design, General Requirements

Sec. 2407

(i) Empirical design of Masonry. 1. General: These empirical procedures may be used for the design or construction of masonry buildings located in those portions of Seismic Zones No. 0 and 1 as defined in Part III of Chapter 23 where the basic wind speed is less than 80 miles per hour as defined in Part II of Chapter 23, subject to approval of the building official. These empirical procedures may be used in lieu of Sections 2406, 2408, 2409, 2410, 2411, 2412 and 2413.

4. Compressive stresses. A. General: Compressive stresses in masonry due to vertical dead loads plus live loads (excluding wind or seismic loads) shall be determined in accordance with this code with permitted live loads reduction.

B. Allowable stresses. The compressive stresses in Masonry shall not exceed the value set forth in Table No. 24-H. The allowable stresses given in Table No. 24-H for the weakest combination of the units and mortar in any load wythe shall be used for all loaded wythes of multi wythes walls.

C, Stresses calculations. Stresses shall be calculated based on specified rather than n nominal dimensions. Calculated compressive stresses shall be determined by dividing the design load by the gross sectional area of the member. The area of openings, chases or recesses in walls shall not be included in the gross cross sectional area of the wall.

D. Anchor bolts. Bolt value shall not exceed those set forth in Table No. 24-M.

5. Lateral support. Masonry walls shall be laterally supported in either the horizontal or vertical direction not exceeding the intervals set forth in Table No. 24-1. Lateral support shall be provide by cross walls, pilasters, buttresses or structural framing members horizontally or by floors, roof or structural members vertically.

Except for parapet walls, the ratio of height to

nominal thickness for cantilever walls shall not exceed 6 for solid masonry and 4 for hollow masonry. The ratio of unsupported height to thickness or the ratio of unsupported length to thickness (one or the other but not both) for solid masonry walls or bearing partitions shall not exceed 20, and shall not exceed 18 for walls of hollow masonry or cavity walls.

In computing the ratio for cavity walls, the value of thickness shall be the sums of the nominal thickness of the inner and outer wythes of the masonry. In walls composed of different classes of units and mortars, the ratio of height or length to thickness shall not exceed that allowed for the weakest combination of units and mortar of which the members is composed.

6. Minimum thickness. A. General. The nominal thickness of masonry bearing walls in buildings more than one story in height shall not be less than 8 inches. Solid masonry walls in one story buildings may be of 6 inches nominal thickness when not over 9 feet in height, provided than when gable construction is used, an additional 6 feet is permitted to the peak of the gable.

(j) Glass Masonry. 1. General. Masonry of glass blocks may be used in non load bearing exterior or interior walls and shall conform to the requirements of sections 2414. Stresses in glass block shall not be utilized.

2. Mortar joints. Glass block shall be laid in type S or N mortar. Both vertical and horizontal mortar joints shall be at least 1/4 inch and not more than 3/8 inch thick and shall be completely filled.

3. Lateral support. Glass panels shall be laterally supported along each end of the panel. Lateral support shall be provided by panel anchors spaced not more than 16 inches on center or by channels. The lateral support shall be capable of resisting the horizontal design forces determined by Chapter 23 or a minimum of 200 pounds per lineal foot of wall, whichever is greater. The connection shall accommodate movement requirements of section 2407 (j) 6.

4. Reinforcing. Glass Block panels shall have joint reinforcement spaced not more than 16 inches on center and located in the mortar bed joint extending the whole length of the panel. A lapping of longitudinal wires for a minimum of 6 inches is required for joint reinforcement splices. Joint reinforcement shall also be placed in the bed joint immediately below and above openings in the panel. Joint reinforcement shall conform with U.B.C standard No 24-15, Part I. Reinforcement shall consist of not less than 2 parallel longitudinal, galvanized steel wires No. 9 gauge or larger, spaced 2 inches apart, and having welded thereto No 9 or heavier gauge cross wires at intervals not exceeding 8 inches. Joint reinforcement in exterior panels shall not be hot-dip galvanized in accordance with U.B.C Standard No 24-15, Part I.

5. Size of panels. Glass Block panels for exterior walls shall not exceed 144 square feet of unsupported wall surface or 15 feet in any dimension. For interior walls, glass block panels shall not exceed 250 square feet of unsupported area or 25 feet in any dimension.

6. Expansion joints. Glass Block panels shall be provided with 1/2 inch expansion joint at along the sides and top and these joints shall have sufficient thickness to accommodate displacements of the supporting structure, but not less than 3/8 inch. Expansion joints shall be entirely free of mortar and shall be filled with resilient material.

7. Reuse of units. Glass Block units shall not be reused after being removed from an existing panel.

Non-bearing walls.
Sec. 2413.
(a) General. All non-load bearing masonry walls shall be reinforced a specified in Section 2407 (h) 4 B. Fences and interior non-bearing non-shear walls may be of hollow unit masonry construction grouted in cells containing vertical and horizontal reinforcement. Non-bearing walls may be used to carry a superimposed load of not more than 200 pounds per linear foot.

(b) Thickness. Every non-bearing masonry wall shall be constructed and have a sufficient thickness to withstand all vertical loads and horizontal loads, but in no case shall the thickness of the wall be less than the value set forth in Table No 24. P. Plaster shall not be considered in computing the height to thickness ratio, as contributing to the thickness of a wall.

(c) anchorage. All non-bearing walls shall be anchored as required by Section 2310 and Section 2337 (b) 8. Suspended ceiling or other non-structural elements shall not be used to provide anchorage for masonry walls.

Masonry Screen Walls.

Sec. 2414.

(a) **General.** Masonry units may be used in non-bearing decorative walls. Units may be laid up in panels with units on edge with the open pattern of the unit exposed in the completed wall.

(b) **Horizontal forces.** The panels shall be capable of spanning between supports to resist the horizontal forces specified in Chapter 23. Winds loads shall be based on gross projected area of the block.

(c) **Mortar joints.** Horizontal and vertical joints shall not be less than 1/4 inch thick. All joints shall be completely filled with mortar and shall be "shoved joint" work. The units of the panel shall be arranged that either the horizontal or the vertical joint containing reinforcing is continuous without offset, this continuous joint shall be reinforced with a minimum of 0.03 square inch of reinforcing steel. Reinforcement may be embedded into mortar.

(d) **Reinforcing.** Joint reinforcing may be composed of 2 wires made with welded ladder or trussed cross ties. In calculating the resisting capacity of the system, compression and tension in the spaced wires may be utilized. Ladder wire reinforcing shall not be spliced and shall be the widest that the mortar joint will accommodate, allowing 1/2 inch of mortar cover.

(e) **Size of panels.** The maximum size of panel shall be 144 square feet, with the maximum dimension in either direction of 15 feet.

(f) **Panel support.** Each panel shall be supported

on all edges by a structural member of concrete, masonry or steel. Supports at the top and end of the panel shall be by means of confinement of the masonry by at least 1/2 inch into and between the flanges at a steel channel. The space between the end of the panel and the web of the panel shall be at least 1/2 inch and shall be void of mortar and shall be filled with resilient material. The use of equivalent configuration in other steel section or in masonry or concrete is acceptable.

Lateral force on Elements of Structures and Non-Structural Components supported by Structures

Section 2336.

(a) General. Parts and portions of structures and their attachments, permanent non-structural components and their attachments, and the attachments for permanent equipment supported by a structure shall be designed to resist the total seismic forces prescribed in Section 2336 (b).

For applicable forces in connectors for exterior panels and diaphragms, refer to Section 2337 (b) 4 and 9.

Forces shall be applied in the horizontal directions, which result in the most critical loadings for design.

(b) Design for Total Lateral Forces: The total design lateral seismic force, F_p, shall be determined from the following formula:

$$F_p = ZIC_pW_p \qquad (36\text{-}1)$$

The values of Z and I shall be the values used for the building.

Exceptions:

1. For anchorage of machinery and equipment required for life-safety systems, the value of *I* shall be taken as 1.5.

2. For the design of tanks and vessels containing sufficient quantities of highly toxic or explosive substances to be hazardous to the safety of the general public if released, the value of *I* shall be taken as 1.5.

3. The value of *I* for panel connectors for panels in Section 2337 (b) 4C shall be 1.0 for the entire connector.

The coefficient C_p is for elements and components and for rigid and rigidly supported equipment. Rigid or rigidly supported equipment is defined as having a fundamental period less than or equal to 0.06 second.

The lateral forces is calculated for non-rigid or flexibly supported equipment supported by a structure and located above grade shall be determined considering the dynamic properties of both the equipment and the structure which supports it, but the value shall not be less than that listed in Table No. 23-P. In the absence of an analysis or empirical data, the value of C_p for non rigid or flexibly supported equipment located above grade on a structure shall be taken as twice the value listed in Table No. 23-P , but not to exceed 2.0.

Exception: Piping, ducting and conduit systems which are constructed of conductible material;s and connections may use the values of C_p from Table No. 23-P.

The value of C_p for elements, components and equipment laterally self-supported at or below ground level may be two thirds of the value set forth in Table No. 23-P. However, the design lateral forces for an element or component or piece of equipment shall not be less than would be obtained by treating the item as an independent structure and using the provisions of Sections 2338.

The design lateral forces determined using Formula(36-1) shall be distributed in proportion to the mass distribution of the element or component. Forces determined using Formula(36-1) shall be used to design members and connections which transfer these forces to the seismic-resisting systems.

(c) Specifying Lateral Forces. Design specifications for equipment shall either specify the design lateral forces prescribed herein or reference these provisions.

(d) Essential or Hazardous Facilities and Life-Safety Systems. For equipment in facilities assigned to Occupancy Categories I and II and for life safety systems, the design and detailing of equipment which needs to be functional following a major earthquake shall consider the effect of drift.

(e) Alternative Designs. Where an approved national standard or approved physical test data provide a basis for the earthquake resistant design of a particular type of equipment or other non-structural component, such a standard or data may be accepted as a basis for design of the items with the following limitations:

1. These provisions shall provide minimum values for the design of the anchorage and the members and connections which transfer the forces to the seismic-resisting system.
2. The force, F_p, and the overturning moment used in the design of the non-structural component

shall not be less than 80 percent of the values that would be obtained using these provisions.

Attachments shall include anchorages and required bracing. Friction resulting from gravity loads shall not be considered to provide resistance to seismic forces.

When the structural failure of the lateral force-resisting systems of non-rigid equipment would cause a life hazard, such system shall be design to resist the seismic forces prescribed in Section 2336 (b).

EXCEPTION: Equipment weighing less than 400 pounds, furniture or temporary or movable equipment.

When allowable design stresses and other acceptance criteria are not contained in or referenced by this code or the U.B.C Standards, such criteria shall be obtained from approved national Standards.

Table No.24-J- Wall lateral support requirements for empirical design of masonry

CONSTRUCTION	MAXIMUM l/t or h/t
Bearing Walls Solid or Solid Grouted All other	20 18
Non-bearing walls Exterior Interior	18 36

Table No 24-H-Allowable compressive stresses for empirical design of masonry

CONSTRUCTION: COMPRESSIVE STRENGTH OF UNIT, GROSS AREA	ALLOWABLE COMPRESSIVE STRESSES[1] GROSS CROSS-SECTIONAL AREA	
	Type M or S Mortar	Type N Mortar
Solid masonry of brick and other solid units of clay or shale; sand-lime or concrete brick:		
8000 plus, psi	350	300
4500 psi	225	200
2500 psi	160	140
1500 psi	115	100
Grouted masonry, of clay or shale; sand-lime or concrete:		
4500 plus psi	275	200
2500 psi	215	140
1500 psi	175	100
Solid masonry of solid concrete masonry units:		
3000 plus psi	225	200
2000 psi	160	140
1200 psi	115	100
Masonry of hollow load-bearing units:		
2000 plus psi	140	120
1500 psi	115	100
1000 psi	75	70
700 psi	60	55
Hollow walls (cavity or masonry bonded)[2] solid units:		
2500 plus psi	160	140
1500 psi	115	100
Hollow units	75	70
Stone ashlar masonry:		
Granite	720	640
Limestone or marble	450	400
Sandstone or cast stone	360	320
Rubble stone masonry		
Course, rough or random	120	100
Unburned clay masonry	30	-----

[1]. Linear interpolation may be used for determining allowable stresses for masonry units having compressive strengths which are intermediate between those given in the table

[2]. Where floor and roof loads are carried upon one wythe, the gross cross-sectional area is that of the wythe under load. If both wythes are loaded, the gross cross-sectional area is that of the minus the area of the cavity between the wythes.

2. Standard Specifications.

Division 4. Masonry. Section 04270, Glass Unit Masonry.

PART 1. GENERAL.

1.00. Related Documents:

A. Drawings and general provisions of the project. Division 1 requirements and conditions to apply to this section.

1.01. Summary:

A. Extent and/or location of glass masonry units.
B. Type of installation; interior; panel anchored; perimeter chase (channels).

1.02. Related work:

A. Mortar - see section 04100.
B. Sealant - see section 07900.
C. Lintel - Metal - see section 05500.
D. Others: sills, flashing, window inserts (if any).

1.03. Submittals:

A. Products data. Provide manufacturer's data for glass units (see section 01300). Includes research reports, fire rating tests...
B. Products data for accessories of installation.
C. Submit samples of glass block requested.
D. Submit mock-up panel or sample panel consisting of 4 glass block preset with color range if necessary.
E. Structural calculations - shop drawing. Furnish as required by architect.

1.04. References:

Provide a reference list of standards.

A. Mortar: ASTM C 780 and ASTM C 270.
B. Portland cement: ASTM C 150, Type I and II.
C. Lime: ASTM C 207, Type S.
D. Aggregate for masonry mortar: ASTM C 144, natural sand.
E. Zinc coating (hot galvanized) for steel products and accessories: ASTM C 123 and ASTM A 153, Class B2.
F. Fire test of window assembly: ASTM E 163.

1.03: Quality assurance and qualifications:

A. Installer and workmanship> Minimum years of experience documented if required or list of references.
B. Guaranty.

1.06. Delivery, storage and handling:

A. Deliver product to site preventing breakage and chipping. Keep in boxes until use.
B. Storage of dry units in a dry and cool area, off the ground, covered for protection against rain, snow and elements. Prevent from staining by other materials contact and mixture.
C. Protect cementitious materials and metal accessories from deterioration or corrosion by moisture and other causes.

1.07. Project conditions:

A. Maintain materials and working conditions to a minimum of 40 to 50 degrees Fahrenheit (4 to 10 degrees Celsius) prior and 48 hours after completion of work.

1.08. Field requirements:

A. Performance bond (if required).
B. Submit other requirements for each special item related to project.

PART 2. PRODUCTS.

2.01. Acceptable manufacturer:

List acceptable manufacturer(s) or equivalent or substitute.

A. Hollow glass block unit. Non-load bearing blocks made of colorless pressed glass, with interior partial vacuum and exterior standard coating factory applied, with or without fibrous insert, corner unit, end block.
B. Solid glass block unit(see manufacturing). One piece solid glass.
C. Nominal and actual size used.
D. Color or tint (bronze...).
E. Pattern and design.
F. Insulation value, compressive strength, light transmission, shading coefficient, sound loss.

2.02. Mortar material:

A. Portland cement: ASTM C 150, type I, low alkali.
B. Lime: ASTM C 207, Type S.
C. Sand: ASTM C 144.
D. Water: drinkable and fresh.
E. Waterproofer.

2.03. Accessories:

A. Panel reinforcing: hot galvanized ladder type welded wire, consisting of 2 parallel side rods of 9 gauge at 1 5/8 inches to 2 inches on center, depending upon thickness used. Cross wires at 8 inches on center.

B. Expansion strip: either glass fiber or polyethylene, density 4-1b, 3/8 inch thick in strip or rolls.

C. Panel anchor: 20 gauge perforated steel strip with punched elongated holes, hot dip galvanized. 0.0359 inch thickness.

D. Perimeter chase or channel if required, according to thickness of glass block used.

E. Asphalt emulsion: water based asphalt emulsion (Karnak 100 mostly specified and used). ASTM D 1187.

F. Packing: polyethylene foam, neoprene or equivalent used for lateral cushioning>

G. Sealant. as specified in section 07900.

H. Color pigment: pure mineral oxides, lime and alkali proof, to produce color to mortar when desired.

I. Miscellaneous materials: dovetails, shims or other.

PART 3. EXECUTION.

3.01. Examination - Inspection:

A. Examine surrounding material opening (sills, head and jamb). Approve surface to receive glass units. Do not proceed to installation until conditions and measurements are satisfactory.

3.02. Preparation:

A. Work shall be plumbed, squared, leveled and straight. Make level lines and marks.
B. Protect areas surrounding the work.

3.03. Installation:

A. Locate and secure channels if any.
B. Apply heavy coat of asphalt emulsion to sill. Allow to dry.
C. Adhere expansion strips to jambs and head of panel using gobs of asphalt emulsion.
D. Set full mortar bed joint to sill.
E. Set lower course of glass blocks. Maintain at all times, horizontal and vertical accurate joint width of 1/4 to 3/8 inch, unless otherwise indicated.
F. Keep expansion joint at jambs and head free of mortar.
G. Place and embed metal anchor and reinforcing rods at first course, then every 24 inches unless otherwise indicated, and before last course occurs, and also immediately above any opening. Overlapping shall not be less than 6 inches. Discontinue reinforcing at expansion joints.
H. Maintain all levels at all times, and until panel is dry.
I. Set succeeding courses of blocks. Maintain proper joint width. Do not furrow mortar. Use wedge if necessary to maintain balance and level and to prevent mortar to be squeezed out.
J. Remove wedges and/or spacers. Fill voids with mortar. Remove surplus mortar and wipe dry.
K. With jointer, and when mortar is still plastic, before full setting, strike joints smooth and concave.
L. Pack at flanges around perimeter and apply

sealant where needed and required.

3.04. Cleaning:

A. Remove all surplus mortar and wipe off each face of glass blocks.

B. Cleaning may be eased with the use of a scrub brush with stiff bristles, and a damp cloth.

C. Do not use abrasive cleaners or wire brush. Do not scratch units.

3.05. Protection of finished work.

3. General Information.

a) <u>Glass blocks are non-load bearing,</u> therefore not designed to support loads. Deflection of the structure above the glass block or supporting it (such as beams, floors and structural members) shall not exceed L/600, not enough to transmit load to the panel. Expected deflection must be determined. Glass blocks should not be subjected to any loads other than their own weight. They should not be exposed to any constraining forces. Expansion and movement at head and jambs should be provided. Permissible installation are:
 1. "Channel chase"
 2. "Panel anchored"
 3. "Crating" or "Grid"

b) <u>Compressive strength.</u> Despite its attribute as a basic opening in fill, because of their high compressive strength and since the weight of the glass block themselves may be neglected, they contribute to reinforce surrounding members so they will withstand wind loads, horizontal live loads and impact loads as well as moderate earthquake. Depending on manufacturer and type of glass block used, numbers vary:

  400 to 850 lbf/in²   P.S.I (Standard)
  2.758 to 5.860 MN/m²   Metric System

of gross bearing area. Average:

  600 lbf/in² or 4.137 MN/m²

Regardless the fact that most manufacturer do not provide all tests and reports, glass blocks, with proper fabrication, would meet the necessary requirements of Chapter 23, Section 2311, Wind Designs and 2336 a and b.

c) <u>Limitations of use.</u> Maximum sizes for panels.

"Uniform Building Code": exterior walls are limited to 144 square feet of unsupported wall surface or 15 feet either side maximum dimension. Interior walls may not exceed 250 square feet of unsupported area or 25 feet either way maximum dimension.

"Basic building Code": exterior walls are limited to 25 feet in length and 20 feet in height between structural supports and/or expansion joints. Area may not exceed 250 square feet. Any panel over 144 sq. ft in area must have supplementary anchorage to structural supports for stiffening. No additional requirements are listed for the limit of interior walls.

"National Building Code" and *"Standard Building Code"*: exterior panels may not exceed 144 sq.ft of unsupported wall surface, or 25 ft in length or 20 ft in height between supports. Interior panels are limited to 250 sq,ft of unsupported area or 25 ft maximum dimension between supports.

D.7: Maximum sizes limit

Building Code (maximum dimensions suggested)		Interior walls			Exterior walls		
		Area Sq.f/m²	Height ft/m	Width ft/m	Area Sq.f/m²	Height ft/m	Width ft/m
Uniform Building Code	4" thick 100 mm	250 / 25	25 / 8	25 / 8	144 / 15	15 / 5	15 / 5
	3" thick 80 mm	150 / 15	20 / 6	25 / 8	85 / 9	10 / 3	25 / 8
Standard Building Code	4" thick 100 mm	250 / 25	25 / 8	25 / 8	144 / 15	15 / 5	15 / 5
	3" thick 80 mm	150 / 15	20 / 6	25 / 8	85 / 9	10 / 3	25 / 8
Basic Building Code		/	/	/	250 * / 25 *	20 / 6	25 / 8

* Panels between 144 and 250 square feet are allowed if they are braced by a special stiffener. (See diagram)

The above information is based for a standard thickness of 4" nominal (190 millimeter). Following table offers both thickness available. The exterior panels sizes are established on a design wind load resistance of 20 lbs/sq.ft and a safety factor of 2.7. Always verify Seismic Requirements of local Building Codes. Same requirements apply, regardless of type of installation (perimeter chase, panel anchor or structural steel insert applications).

D.8: General Physical Properties
(on most common sizes used)

Dimension (nominal)	6 x 6 x 4	8 x 8 x 4	12 x 12 x 4	8 x 8 x 3
U Value Thermal coefficient Heat transmission BTU/Sq.ft x Hrs x F	0.39 to 0.48	0.37 to 0.48	0.36 to 0.48	0.40 to 0.53
R value Thermal resistance Sq.ft x Hrs x F/BTU	2.08 to 2.52	2.08 to 2.64	2.08 to 2.74	2.08 to 1.89
S.T.C Sound Transmission Class	38 to 41	38 to 42	38 to 42	38 to 40
P.S.I Compressive Strength	400 to 650	→	→	→
% Light Transmission	72 to 74	→	→	79 to 82
Shading Coefficient	0.65	0.65	0.63	0.66
Weigh per block	3.5	6.4	10.6	5.4

Note: * Weigh per square foot of glass blocks installed (mortar installation): 20 lbs per sq.ft or 98 kg per M^2 regardless the size of block used (except fire block and solid block)
  * U Coefficient tends to diminish in Summer approximately 0.03 to 0.05.
  * R Coefficient tends to increase in Summer approximately 0.06 to 0.11.

D.9: Conversion tables

(American Standard / Metric System conversion table of most common sizes and measures used through manual and for Glass Block in general)

	American Standards inches "		Metric System millimeters mm	
	Nominal	Actual	Nominal	Actual
Thickness	3 4	3 1/4 3 3 7/8 4 3 1/2	80 100 90	79.38 76.20 98.43 101.60 88.90
Width and Height	4 5 6 8 10 12	3 3/4 3 1/2 4 1/2 5 3/4 5 1/2 5 1/2 7 3/4 7 1/2 9 1/2 11 3/4 11 1/2	95 90 115 150 150 140 200 190 240 300 290	95.25 88.90 114.30 146.05 146.05 139.70 196.85 190.50 241.30 298.45 292.12
Joints, Allowances, etc...		1/8 1/4 3/8 1/2 5/8 3/4		3.12 6.24 9.52 12.49 15.87 18.73

Notes: Maximum size of actual production of Glass Blocks
Glass Blocks are designated as follows:
  Width x Height x Thickness
i.e: 6" x 8" x 3"
  150 mm x 200 mm x 100 mm

1"	=	2.54 cm
1"	=	25.4 mm
1 cm	=	0.3937"
1'0"	=	0.3048 M
1 M	=	39.37"
1 M	=	3'3"
1 lb	=	0.453 kg
1 kg	=	2.205 lbs
1 sq.ft	=	0.1 M^2
1 M^2	=	10.8 sq.ft
1 sq.Y	=	0.9 M^2

d) Curved walls: Minimum radius for curved panels should be guided by the table, information and following illustration. Construction of serpentine walls, round columns or a simple curved shower panel, items tending to be rather popular, should be carefully planed so that a decent vertical grout line appears, knowing it will be clearly distinguished by a constant, neat and **thinner** horizontal joint on at least one side.

Good average workmanship for such assembly, here is more suggested. Vertical grout line on convex side will be more extruded therefore more visible. However, the effect will be tempered when completing a straight "dead" plumb line, smooth and continuous as the eye goes down from block to block.

The standard joint thickness, in mortar installation, varies from 1/4" to 3/8". For curved walls, it should be appropriate at vertical lines and not be wider than 5/8" to 3/4". I have seen rare situations where vertical grout lines had to be 1" and over and I suggested the use if thin tile insert between the blocks: the result was pleasing but it should not be used unless necessary.

There is actually a few manufacturers producing a "radius" block (i.e: "all-bent" from Weck Manufacturing, sold only in 4" x 8" x 4" nominal). It can be adjusted to a small range of radii and it will create an uniform grout line both vertically and horizontally. However, it is available only in the size mentioned above and very costly at purchase.
Where several curves or junction of a curve and straight wall occur a vertical expansion joint (or stiffener) is required, each time there is a change of

direction and/or a section exceeding 18 ft (6 meters).

e) Sizes: Generally, all manufacturers provide the same common sizes, either American standard sizes or metric sizes, or both. The next table shows the basic market availability.

D.10: Minimum radius for curved panels

STANDARD (nominal) inches	METRIC (nominal) mm	Minimum Radius inches	Minimum Radius cm	Joint Thickness in	Joint Thickness out	Number of blocks used in 90° arc
------------	95 x 200 x 95	30"	76cm	1/8	5/8	13
4 x 8 x 4	95 x 200 x 100	32"	81cm			
4 x 8 x 3	95 x 200 x 80	35"	89cm			
5 x 5 x 3	115 x 115 x 80	39"	98cm			
------------	145 x 145 x 100	46"	116cm			
6 x 6 x 4	150 x 150 x 100	48 1/2"	123cm			
6 x 6 x 3	150 x 150 x 80	52"	132cm			
6 x 8 x 3	150 x 200 x 80	52"	132cm			
------------	190 x 190 x 100	63"	160cm			
8 x 8 x 4	200 x 200 x 100	65"	165cm			
8 x 8 x 3	200 x 200 x 80	69"	175cm			
10 x 10 x 3	240 x 240 x 80	80"	203cm			
12 x 12 x 4	300 x 300 x 100	96 1/2"	245cm			

Notes: 1. Thickness here affects minimum radius suggested
2. Only **2** thicknesses of glass block are currently available

	Nominal	Actual	Nominal	Actual
Standard	4"	3 7/8"	100mm	98.42mm
Thin line	3"	2 7/8"	80mm	79.37mm
	American sizes		Metric sizes	

3. There is no limitation on **maximum** radius for curved walls
4. A 90o arc always contains 13 units. regardless the size of the block used
5. When several curves occur (serpentine wall, etc...), a vertical expansion expansion must be provide at each apex (or change of curvature, direction) and every 18' (6 meters).

D.11: Minimum radius for curved panels
(Illustration / not to scale)

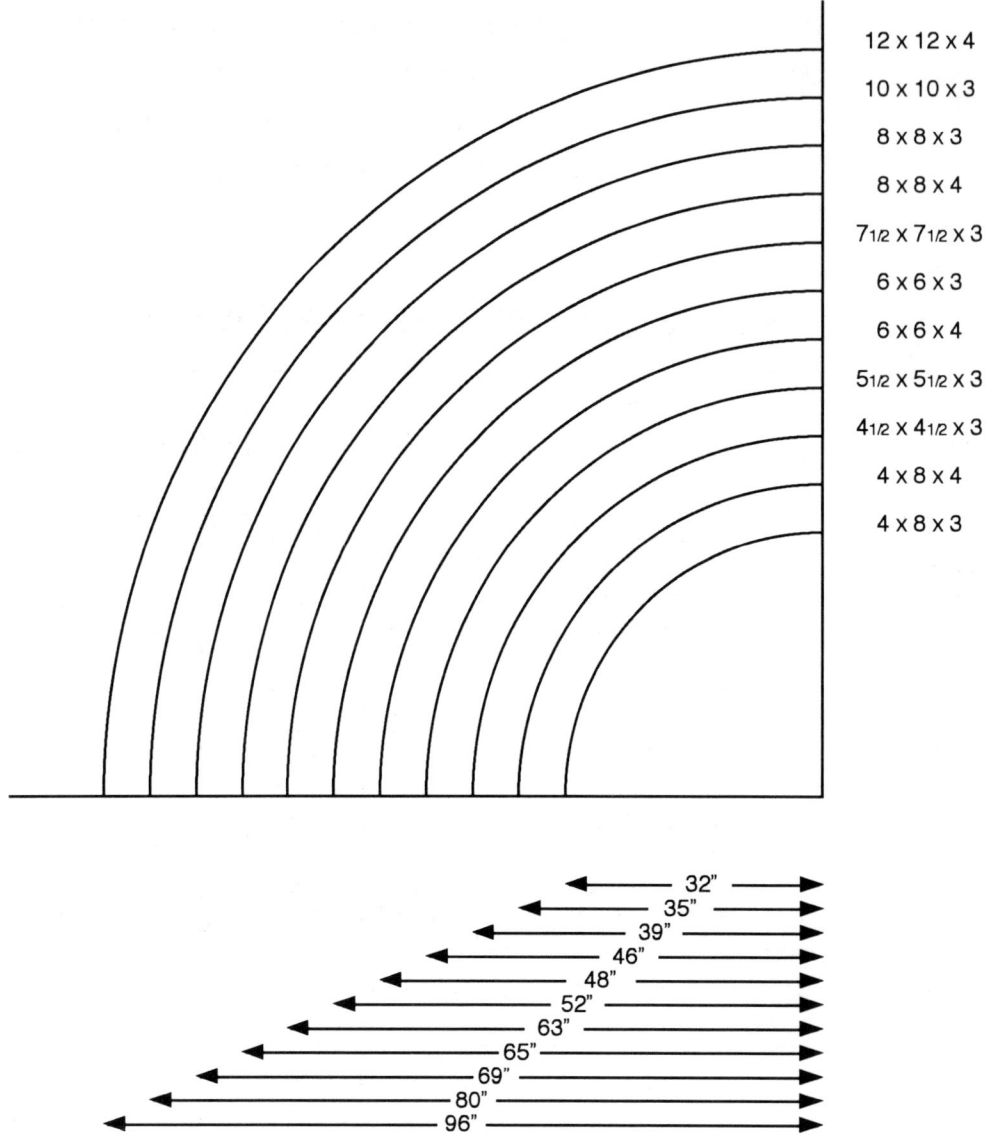

Notes: For metric sizes, refer to previous table and transpose.

D.11: Most common sizes actually available on the market and number of blocks required per square foot and square meter*

Standard (nominal) inches	Metric (nominal) mm	Number of blocks required	
		Per square foot	Per square meter
4 x 8 x 3	95 x 200 x 80	4.5	48
4 x 8 x 4	95 x 200 x 100	4.5	48
5 x 5 x 3	115 x 115 x 80	6.4	68
6 x 6 x 3	150 x 150 x 80	4	43
6 x 6 x 4	150 x 150 x 100	4	43
5 1/2 x 5 1/2 x 3 3/4	140 x 140 x 95	4.4	47
6 x 8 x 3	150 x 200 x 80	3	32
8 x 8 x 3	200 x 200 x 80	2.25	24
8 x 8 x 4	200 x 200 x 100	2.25	24
7 1/2 x 7 1/2 x 3 3/4	190 x 190 x 95	2.4	26
10 x 10 x 3	240 x 240 x 80	1.5	16
6 x 12 x 4	150 x 300 x 100	2	21
1 11/2 x 1 11/2 x 3 3/4	290 x 290 x 80	1.05	12
12 x 12 x 4	300 x 300 x 100	1	11

Notes: Thickness does not affect number per square foot or square meter.
Table is designed for estimates and/or installation purposes.

Kleid Residence
Architect: House + House, Steven House
Photographer: Steven House
Pittsburgh-Corning Decora® Pattern

Alhambra Police Facilities
Architect: Dworsky and Associates
Glass Block Installers

Chapter 7

Details and Finishes

This section will provide architects and contractors with the most commonly encountered applications in residential and commercial constructions. They may vary according to manufacturers and local Building Codes.

Our attention will be first focused on the most used application, and of particular interest to homeowners, in a residential window situation, exterior and interior, less than 144 square feet. This is the maximum size imposed by Building Code, that does not requires expansion or control joint or stiffeners. The following is a step by step method which may be coordinated with the step by step installation dealt with in chapter 9.

First, let's make a few points: unless it is a remodeling project, glass blocks must be installed right after "rough framing", before drywall, and lath and plaster or stucco, and/or before float and tile. Therefore, 3 details prevail, one for jambs (or left and right sides), one for head (top or header) and one for sill (or base/bottom of panel).

Note: you may notice that jambs (sides) and head (top/header) have the same detail and consideration; they **do not** receive any mortar.

* The following diagrams use a standard 8 x 8 x 4 glass block and 2 x 4 metal or wood studs.

* The use of metal studs does not affect the order and details of procedures.

When using 2 x 6 metal or wood studs, guidelines and details varies to allow interior and exterior finishes to return on both sides of the glass block panel perimeter. See figures 7-1a.

Saddleback Animal Care Center
El Toro, California
Glass Block Installers

EXTERIOR DETAILS

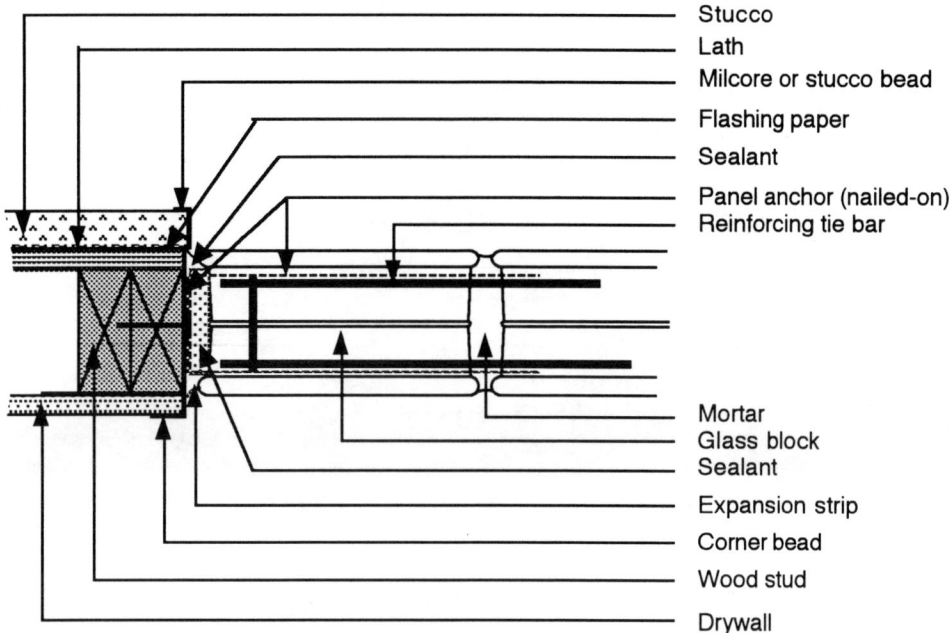

Figure 7-1: Exterior panel jamb detail, wood stud, exterior finish: stucco interior finish: drywall

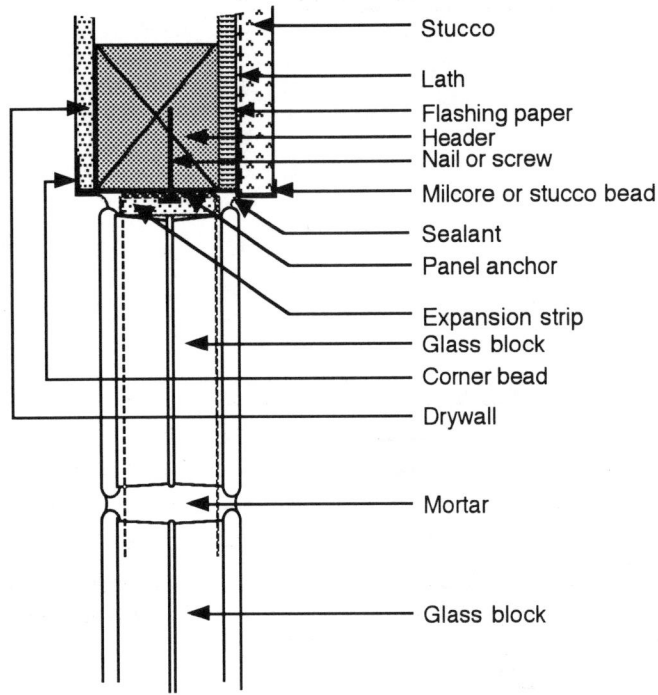

Figure 7-2: Exterior panel head detail, wood stud, exterior finish: stucco interior finish: drywall

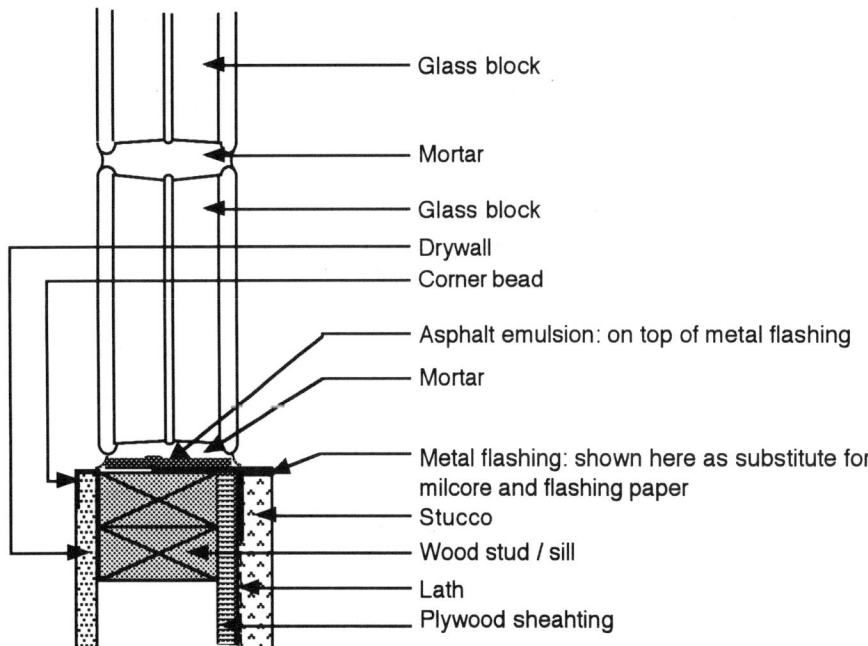

Figure 7-3: Exterior panel sill detail, wood stud, exterior finish: stucco interior finish: drywall

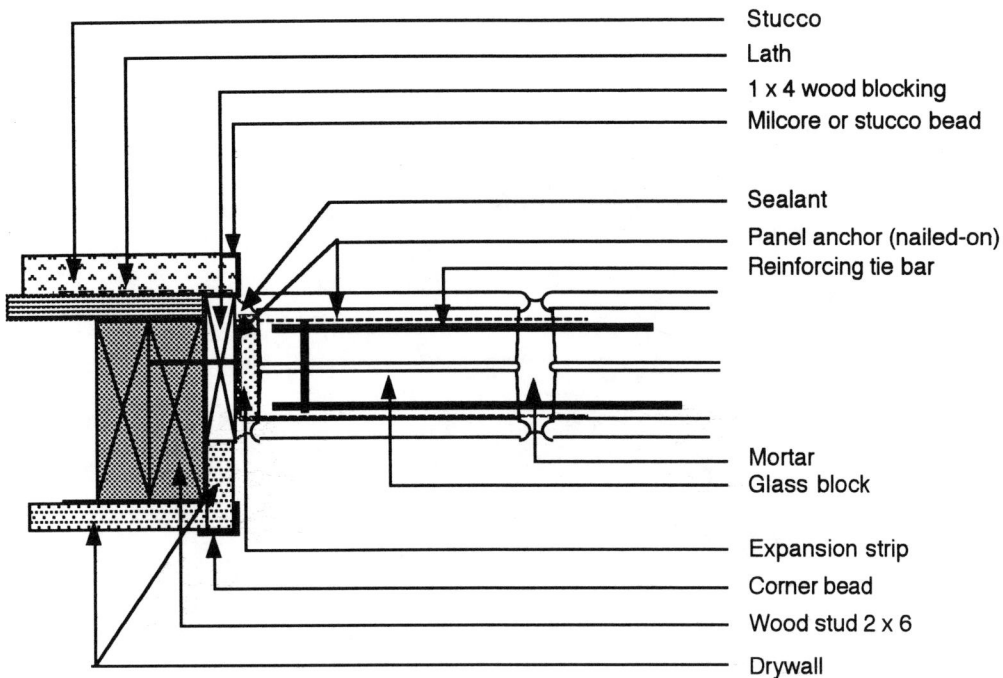

Figure 7-1a: Exterior panel jamb detail, 2 x 6 wood stud, exterior finish: stucco interior finish: drywall

INTERIOR DETAILS

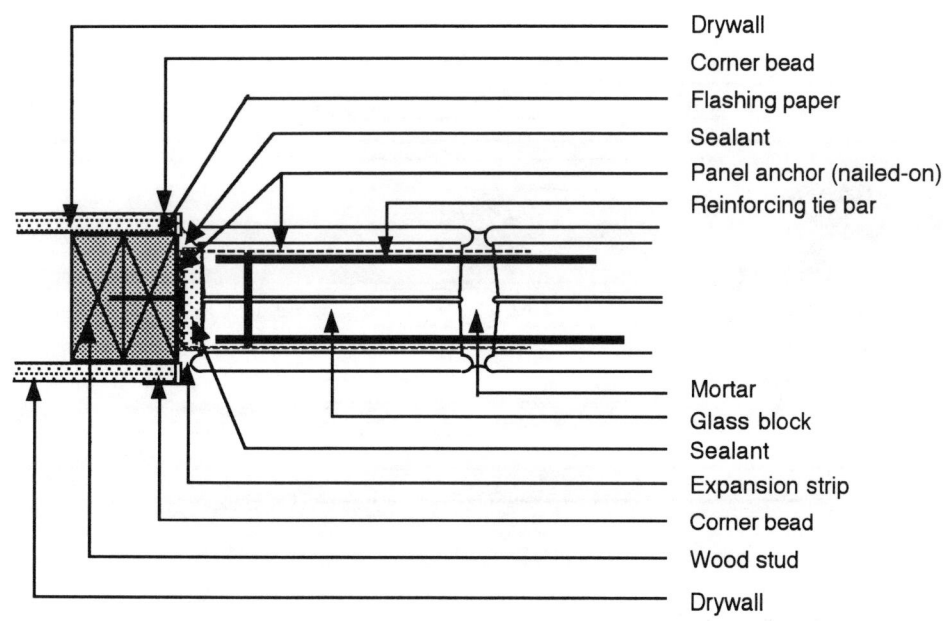

Figure 7-4: Interior panel jamb detail, wood stud, interior finish: drywall both sides

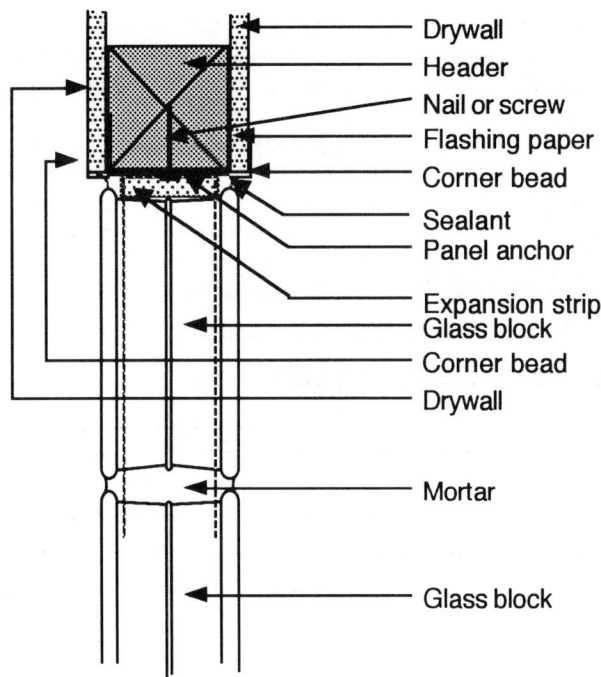

Figure 7-5: Interior panel head detail, wood stud, interior finish: drywall both sides

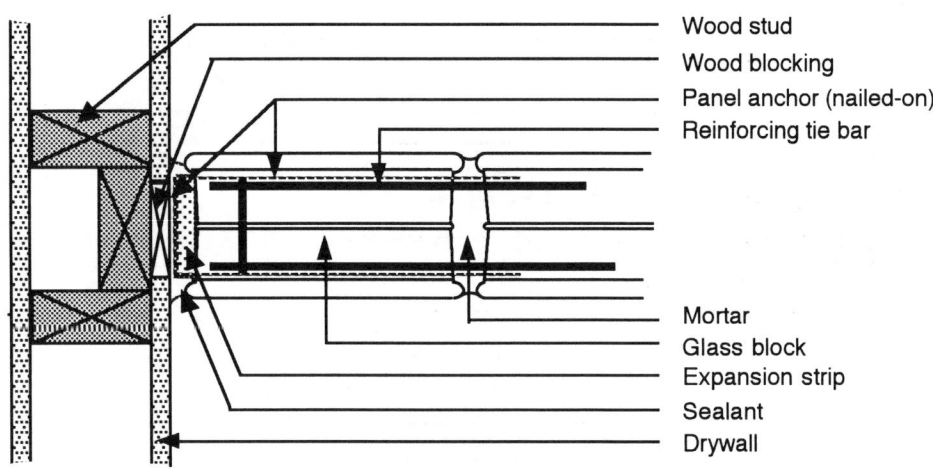

Figure 7-6: Interior panel jamb detail, at partition, wood stud, interior finish: drywall both sides

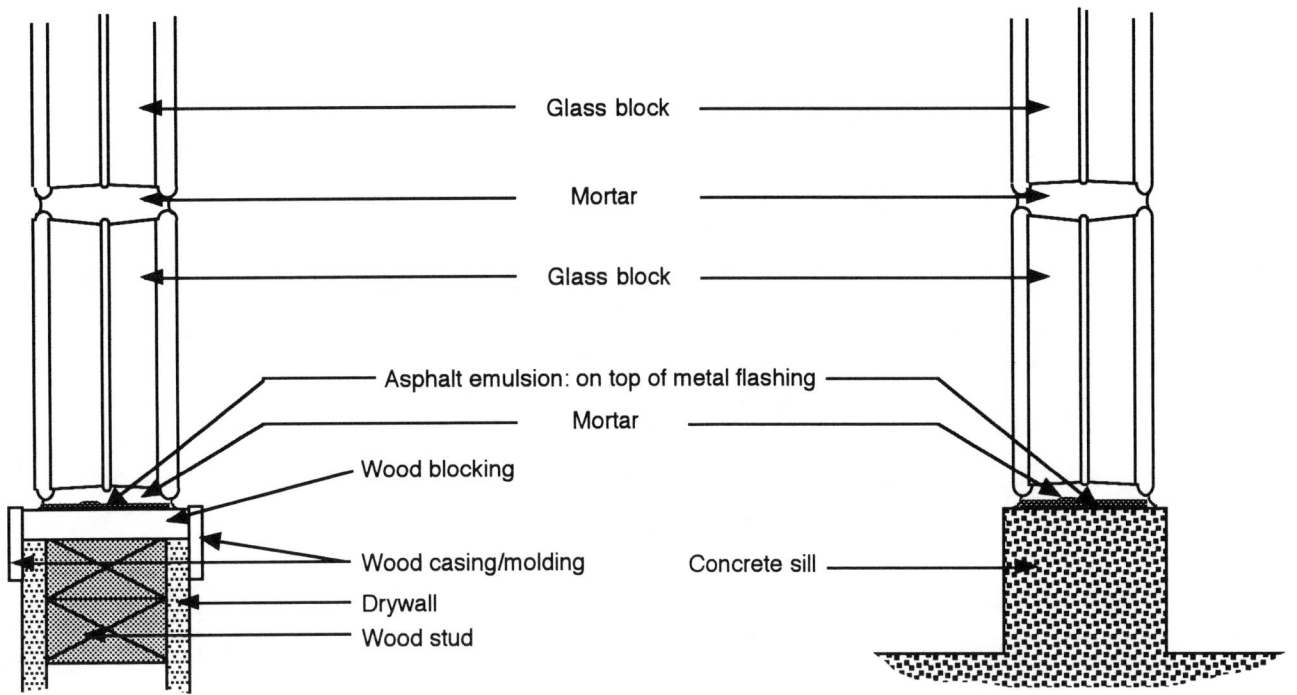

Figure 7-7: Interior panel sill details.

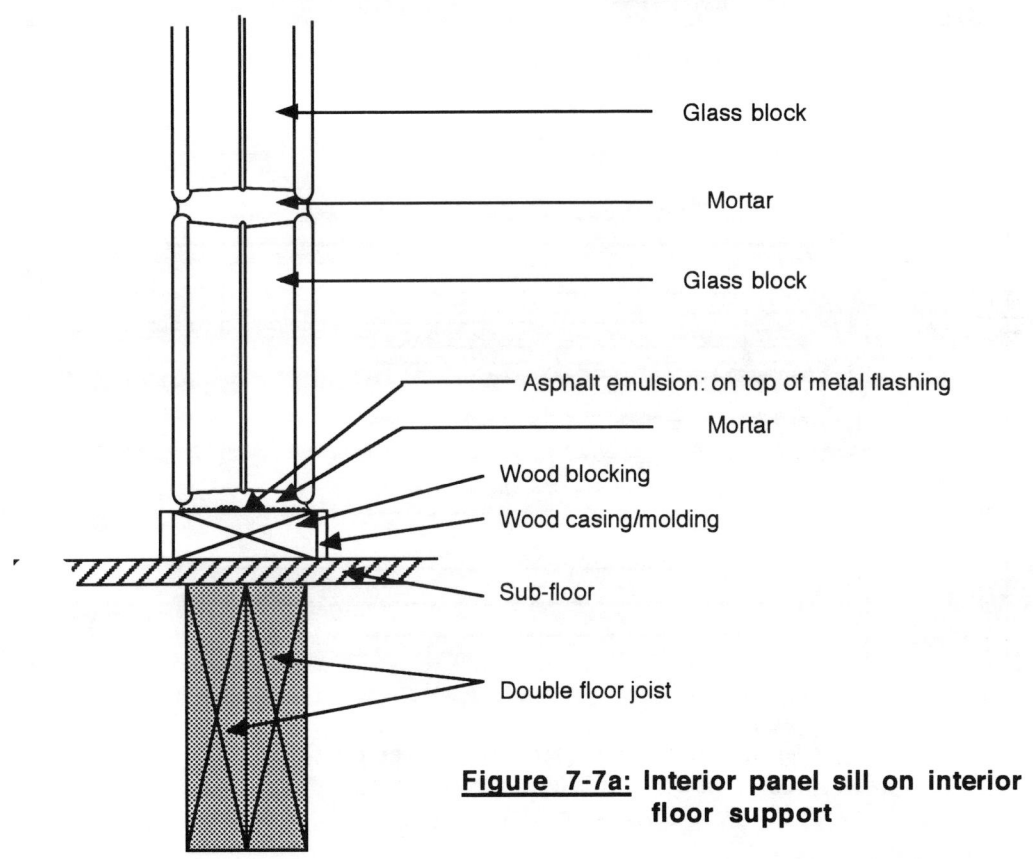

Figure 7-7a: Interior panel sill on interior floor support

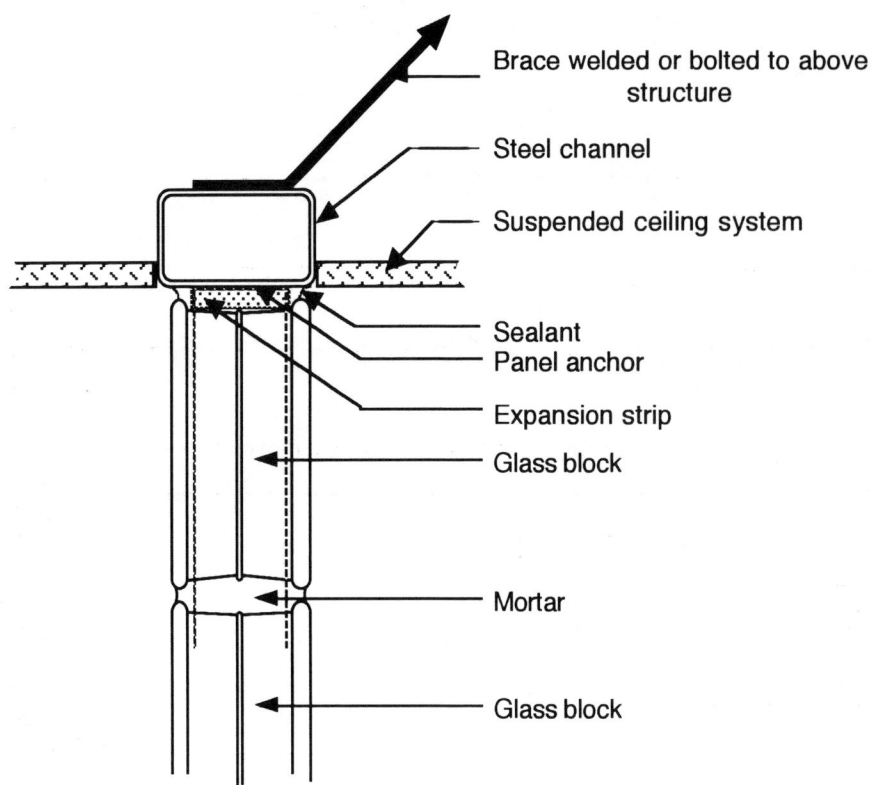

Figure 7-8: Interior panel head detail at suspended ceiling

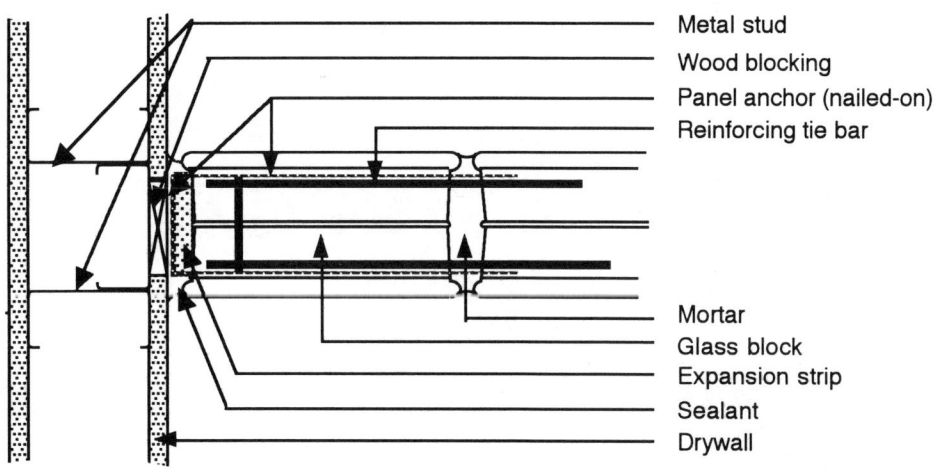

Figure 7-9: Interior panel jamb detail, at partition, metal stud, interior finish: drywall both sides. Sinilar to 7-6

CHANNEL DETAILS

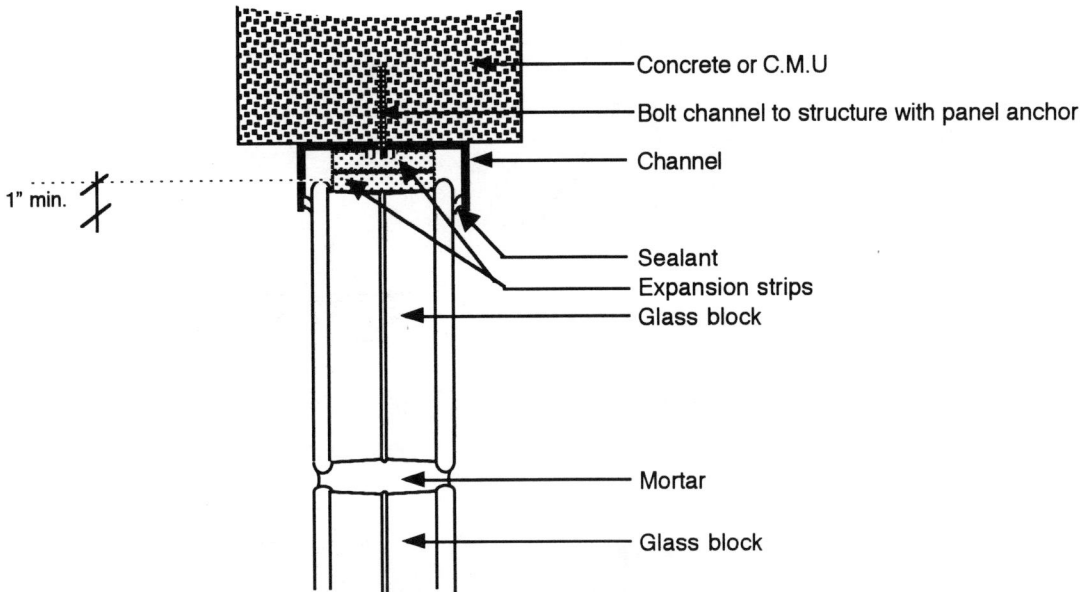

Figure 7-10: Exterior panel head detail
Channel installation
Concrete or C.M.U

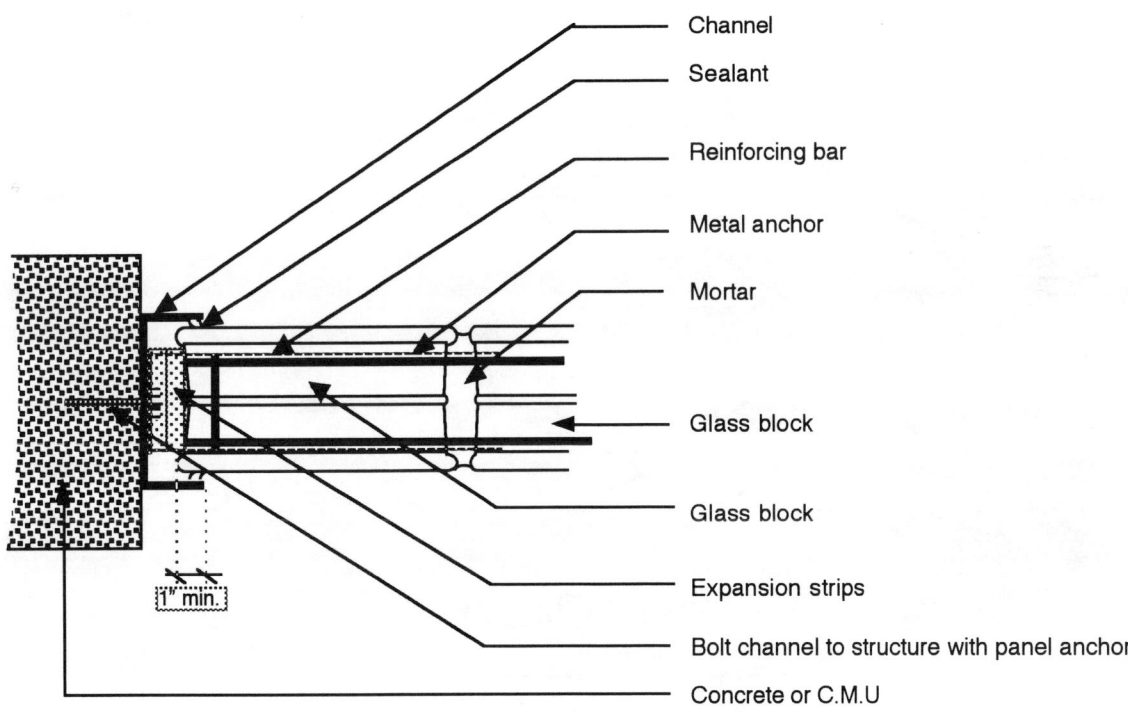

Figure 7-11: Exterior panel jamb detail
Channel installation
Concrete or C.M.U

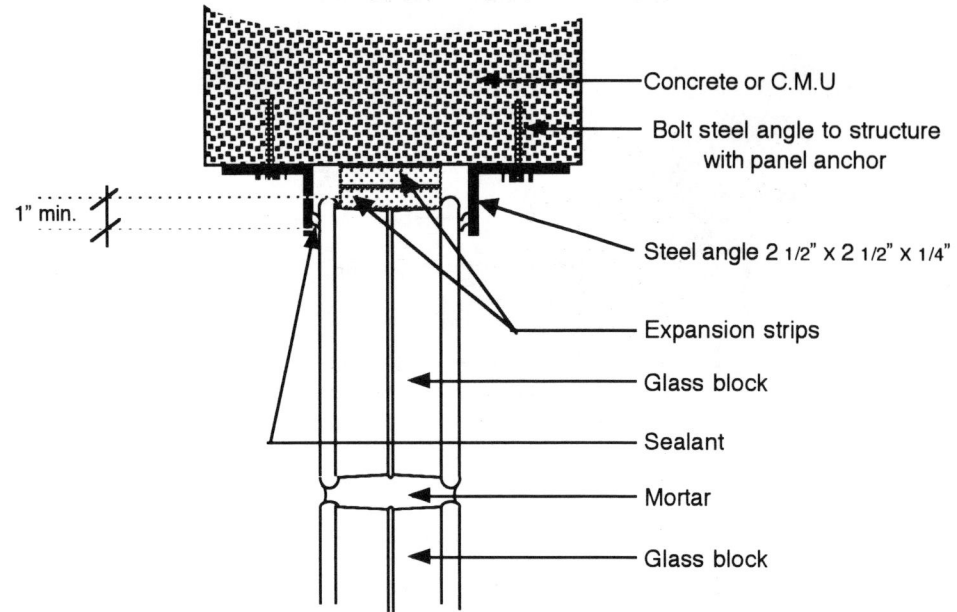

**Figure 7-10a: Exterior panel head detail
Steel angle installation
Concrete or C.M.U**

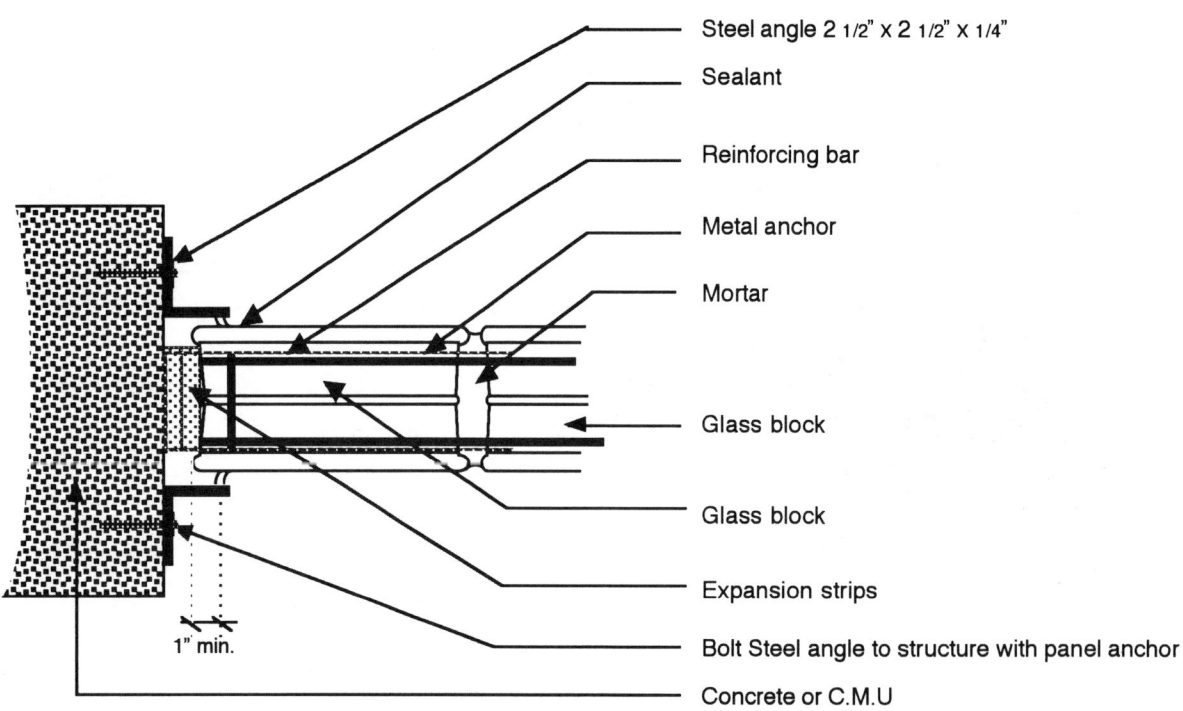

**Figure 7-11a: Exterior panel jamb detail
Steel angle installation
Concrete or C.M.U**

MULTIPLE PANELS

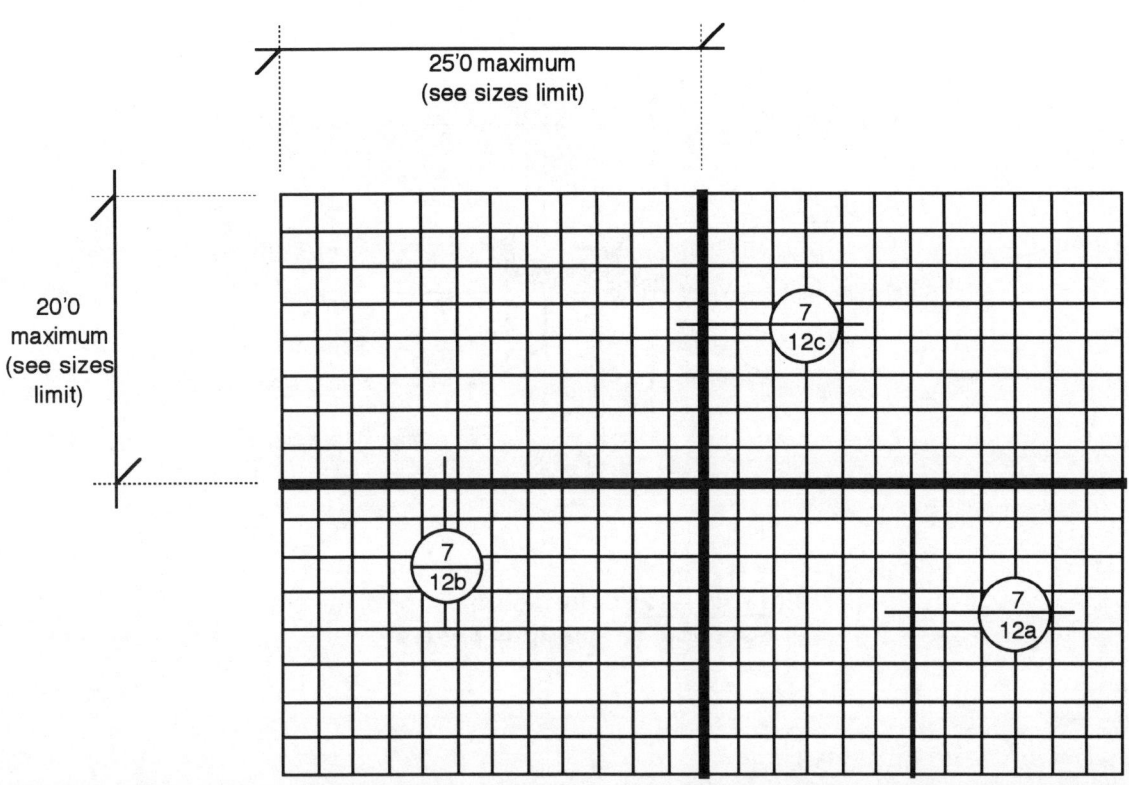

Figure 7-12: Multiple panels

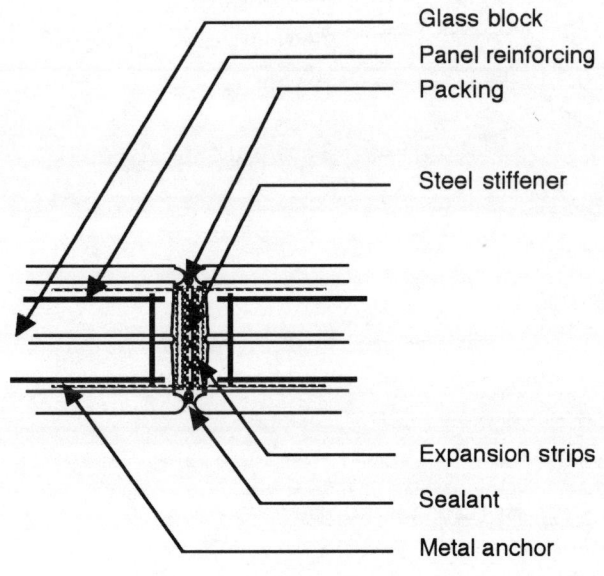

Note: Reinforcement and anchor attachments are interrupted at stiffener. Panels including hidden steel plate joint stiffener should not exceed 10'0 in height.

Figure 7-12a: Stiffener section at multiple panels

page 93

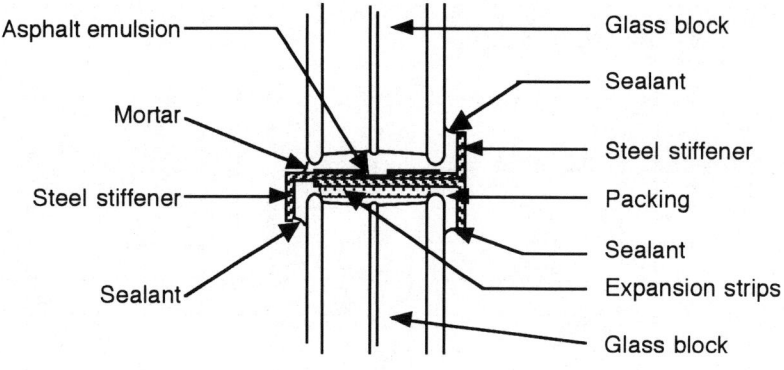

Figure 7-12b: Horizontal support section at multiple panels

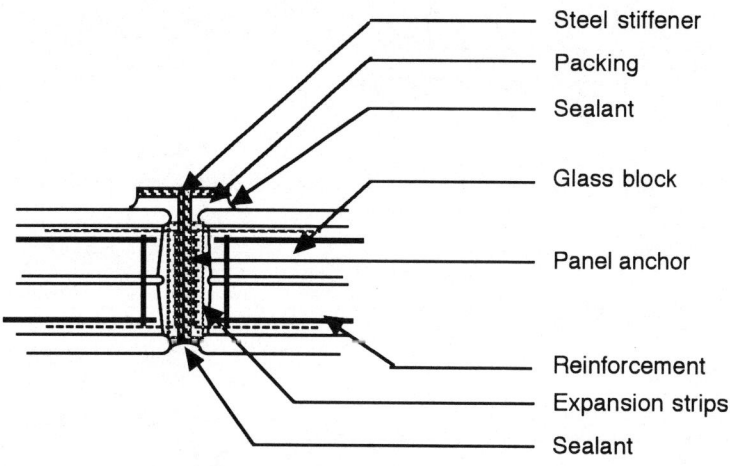

Figure 7-12c: Horizontal support section at multiple panels

MULTIPLE / OVERSIZE PANELS (Alternate)

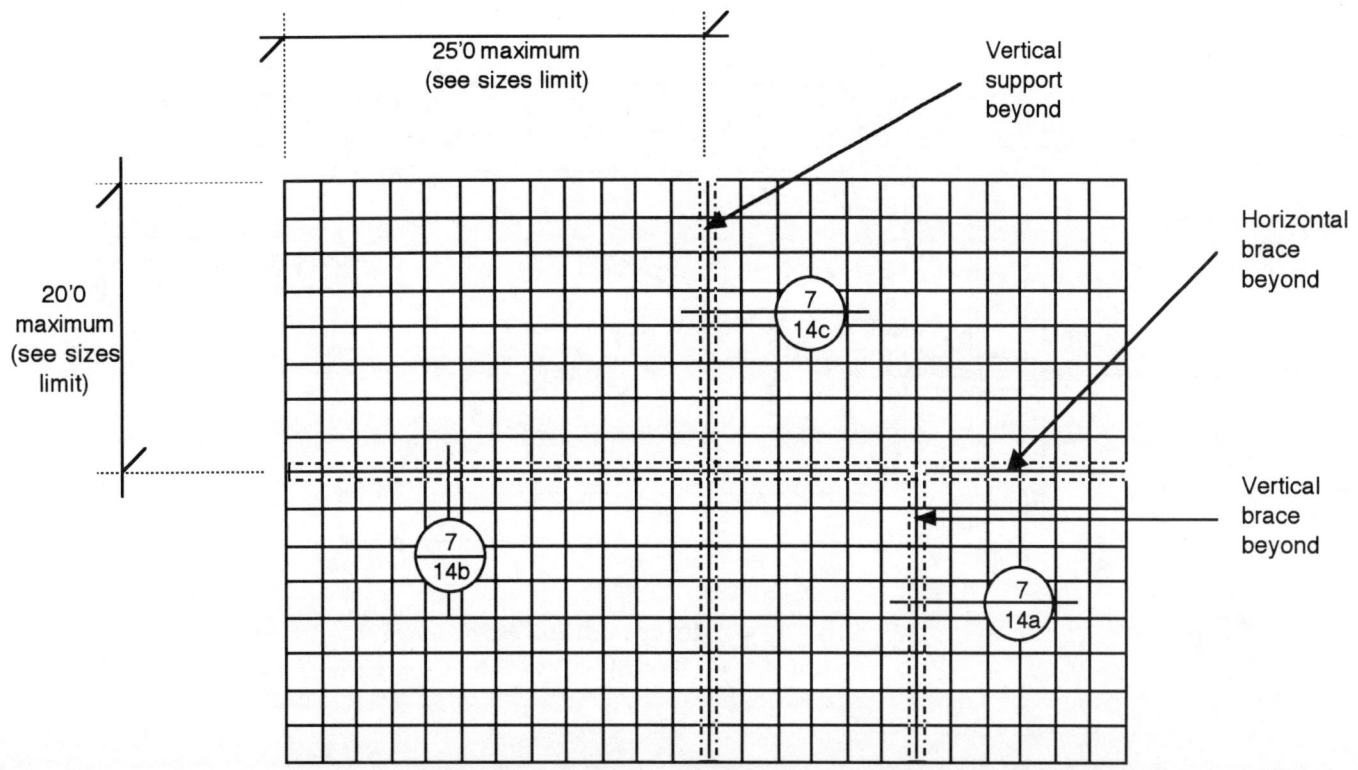

Figure 7-14: Multiple panels

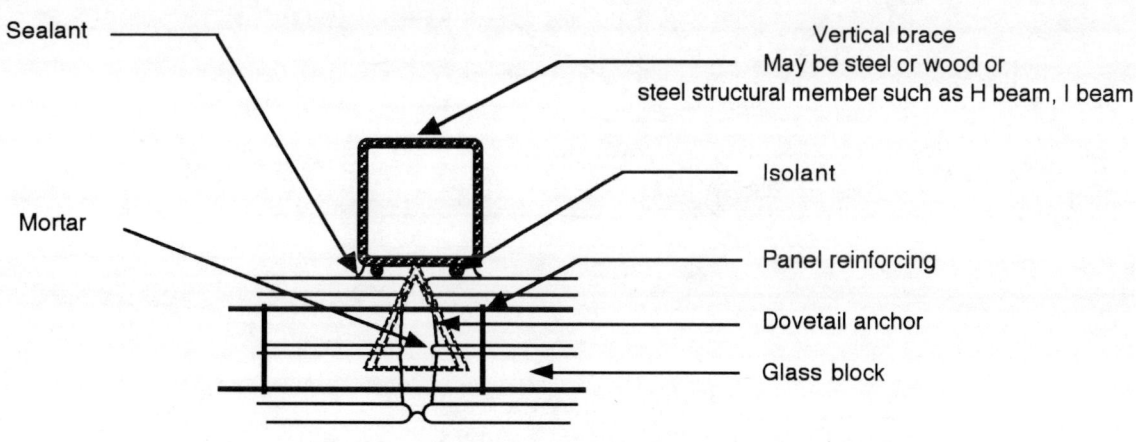

Figure 7-14a: Intermediate vertical brace at oversize panels

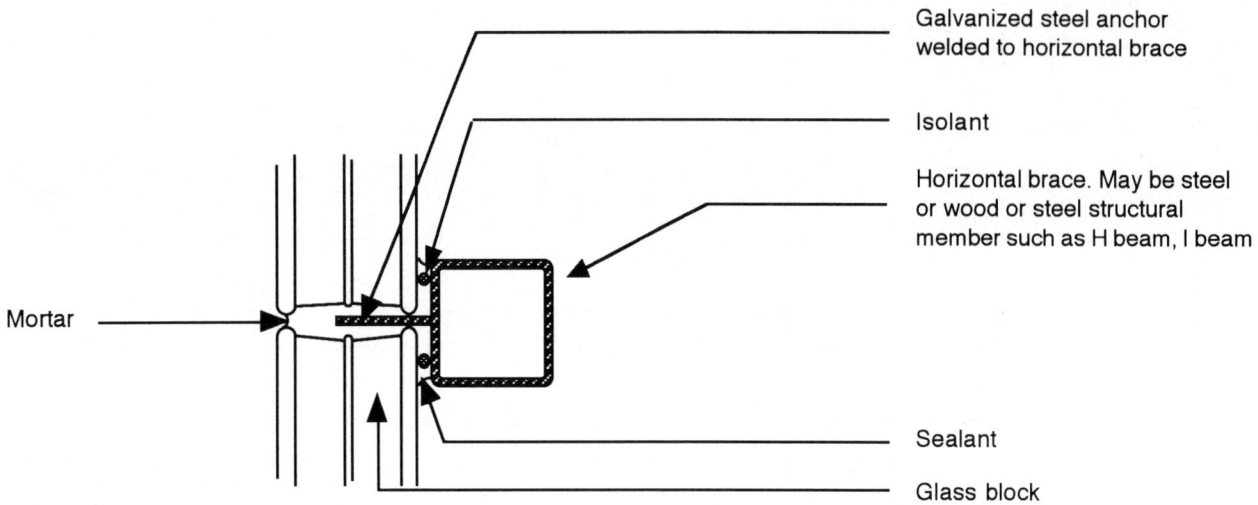

Figure 7-14b: Intermediate horizontal brace at oversize panels

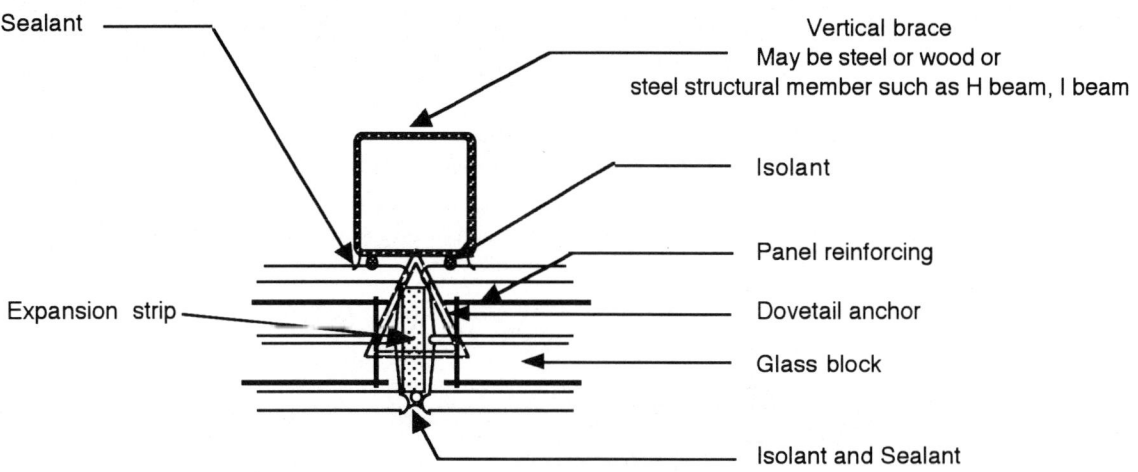

Figure 7-14c: Intermediate vertical support at oversize panels (shown with sealant alternate)

Combination of 4 different sizes
Alan Marino Residence
Los Angeles, California
Glass Block Installers

Chapter 8

Design and Selection

Whether used in a commercial or residential application, glass block is a perfect material to encourage unusual concepts leading to a very personalized statement on the part of the designer for their client. The possibilities are endless. With imagination, this product becomes an attractive tool in creating something out of ordinary.

Vertical wall applications are extremely popular, followed by use on floors, decks, ceilings and skylights. A review of its general and physical properties will give a better understanding and meaning to this chapter. A good knowledge of glass block usage and method of assembly will aid the creative melding with other materials, from both the structural and cosmetic angle. Most suppliers will provide the public with a sometimes limited list of items and accessories for installation that may enlarge realization of ideas.

1. Factors of selection.

The following could be used as a checklist indicating the various advantages and properties of glass blocks as discussed previously, now exposed to contact, functionally and anesthetically at work and at home. In analyzing the outcome of direct and indirect effects, location, size, amount and pattern should be carefully and naturally selected.

(a) Sun exposure:

- Direct and long exposure to the sun (i.e where hitting a work area).
- Solar blocks and light directive blocks may be considered.
- A 10 to 20 degree angle facing north will not affect light transmission.

(b) People exposure:

- In a working area superior illumination. will be required.
- Position of occupant facing a glass block panel for a long period.
- Dense pattern or even sandblasting may be preferred where brightness is excessive.
- Where brightness is desired, the same light directive or clear transparent units will bring a

necessary clarity for better use in a room if exposed to a partially shaded area.

(c) Size of room:

- Refer to limitations of use and local building codes
- Adjust size of panel to size of room, by amount of light needed.

(d) Sound exposure:

- Remember the potent insulation factor.
- Ideal for conference rooms.
- A shower may be imaginatively placed as the divider between master bath and master bedroom.

(e) Fire rating requirements:

- Refer to previous chapter.
- Carefully consult plan and specification of project. Patterns and sizes are limited in special fire rating applications.
- Regular glass blocks have a standard 45 minute rating (for all manufacturers).
- See manufacturers providing 60 minute and 90 minute fire rating units.

2. Pattern selection.

Choice of pattern may be simply guided by:
- Privacy
- Aesthetic: the wide selection of choice as well as patterns should cover most if not everyone's taste.
- Light: amount of light needed (may be controlled by items such as blinds and louvers.

3. Design.

Here, as we mentioned before, creating a design is where your imagination can be let loose. It is interesting to note that once you look around your daily environment, you will find many examples of design that hopefully will give you the impetus to create your own magic. Even the picture in this manual could give you a starting point. I am supplying you a few sketches of the most encountered or requested forms of interior and exterior panels. As well as composing the perimeter line irregularly or symmetrically, you could also combine sizes and patterns with positive and surprising results. It is not suggested to mix manufacturers as some of their mold may vary, as well as the glass "color" (pigmentation). The "greenish" main variation noted from a manufacturer to another may be quite substantial, as each manufacturing components may vary in chemical composition (see "Manufacturing").

A basic knowledge of mathematics should resolve most problem:

A 12 inches square can be made up thus:
6" + 6" or 8" + 4" or 4" + 4" + 4" etc...
A 24 inches square can be made up thus:
12" + 12" or 8" + 4" + 8" + 4"
6" + 6" + 6" + 6" or 8" + 8" + 8" etc...

A good performance is ensured if you have plumbed, uniform and continuous vertical and horizontal grout lines. It may easily be obtained by using the popular plastic spacers, as we will see in the chapter dedicated to installation. You may very well combine several sizes and 2 or more patterns. In

fact, joints should almost look like a drawing.
The following designs of panels are possible with any square size of Glass Blocks (8" x 8", 6" x 6" and 12" x 12"). As to the "step" effect, note that the bigger the block is, the more steep the step will be accentuated. The following drawings illustrate the start of a numerous amount of variations.

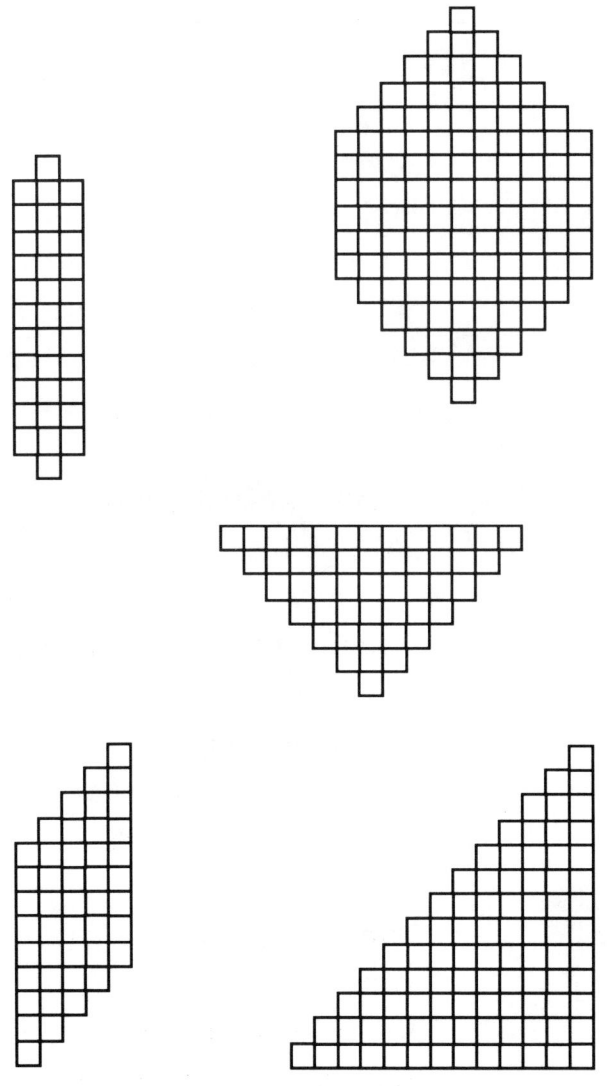

Other possibilities and combinations includes mixing sizes. Two or three patterns (more than three is not suggested) may be mixed as well, provided manufacturer selection and availability. Simple mathematics can generate hundreds of variations such as following.

Using......

12" x 12"   and   6" x 12"

Using......

12" x 12"   and   6" x 6"

Design composition
Residence
Glass Block Installers

Using......

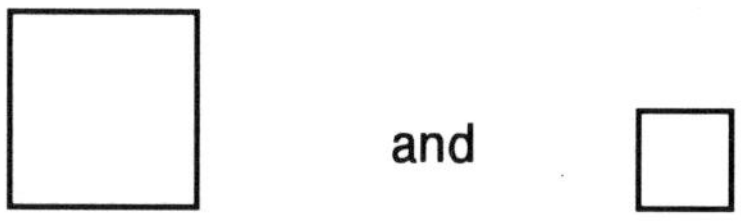

12" x 12"   and   6" x 6"

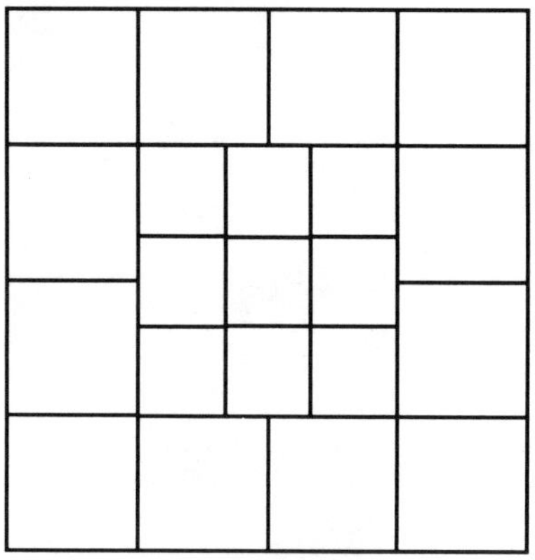

Using......

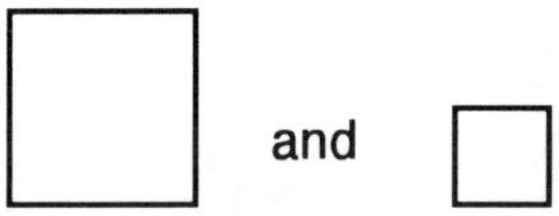

12" x 12"   and   6" x 6"

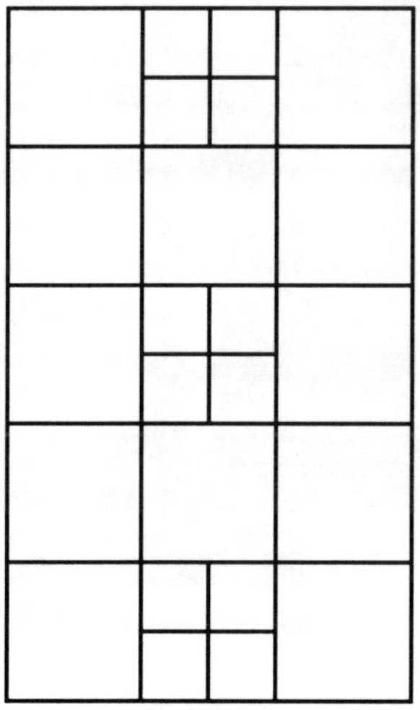

Using......

8" x 8"
or
12" x 12"
or
6" x 6"

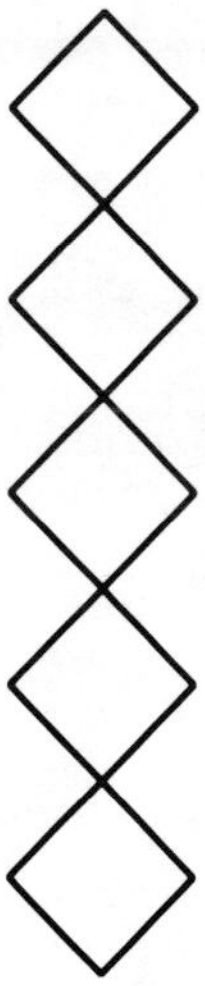

page 105

Design composition
Commercial office
Glass Block Installers

Using......

12" x 12"   and   6" x 6"

Using......

12" x 12"   6" x 6"   8" x 8"

page 107

Design composition
Dr Leroy Perry Sports Medicine Center
West Los Angeles, California
Glass Block Installers

Design composition
Dr Leroy Perry Sports Medicine Center
West Los Angeles, California
Glass Block Installers

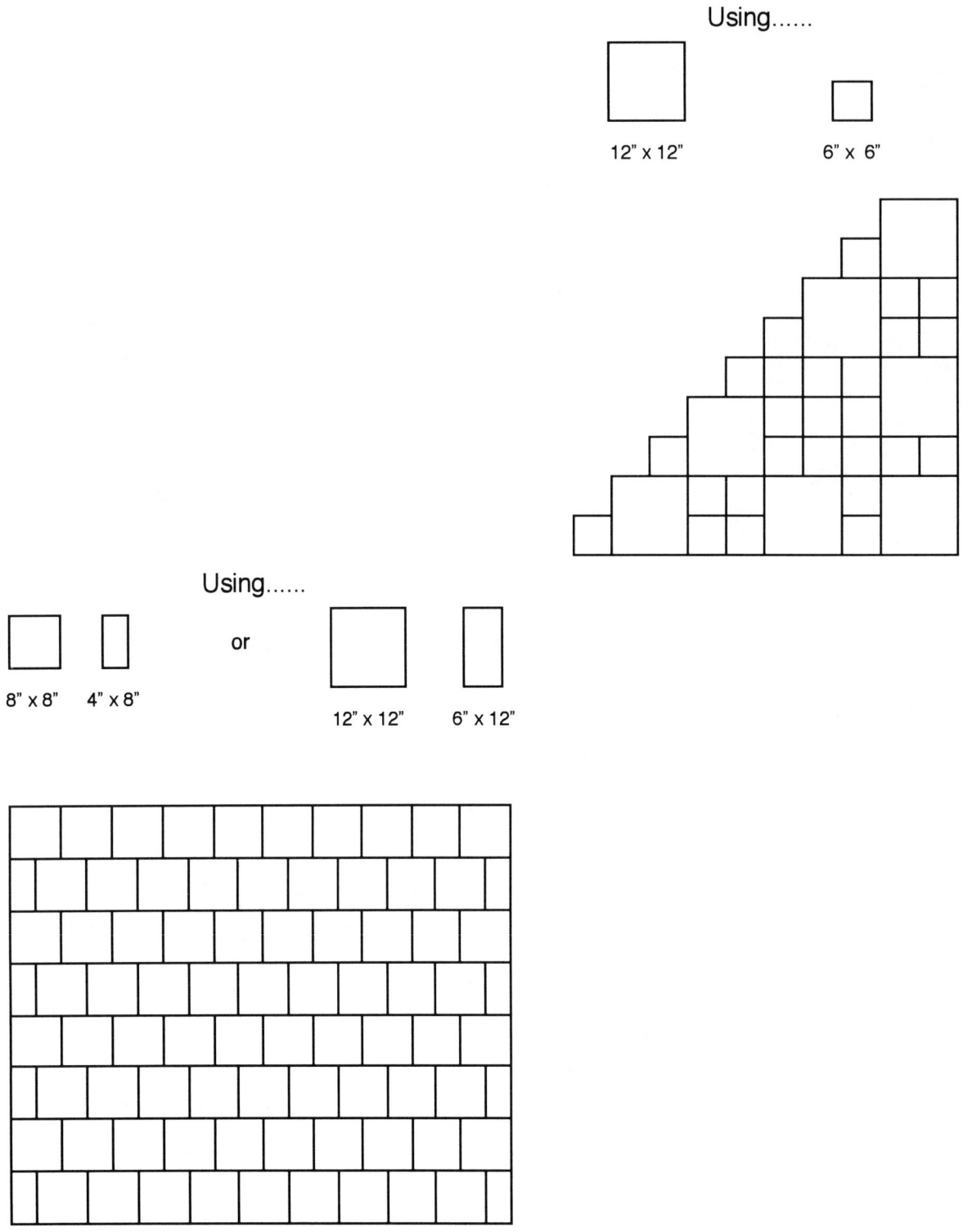

Using......

12" x 12"   6" x 6"

Using......

8" x 8"   4" x 8"   or   12" x 12"   6" x 12"

Brick pattern

Using......

12" x 12"   and   6" x 6"

Using wall covering construction methods, the following panels may be achieved using systems that will be described and discussed in the chapter dedicated to installations:

1. By cutting the glass block following the line designated and inserting it into a custom channel preinstalled at the perimeter.

2. By erecting the wall beyond the final finish line conveyed and dropping the finish material (drywall, wood paneling...) on top of each side of the glass block panel and caulking the edges where dissimilar materials meet (steel channel and glass block).

These methods open new limits and another wide range to performance in design, creation and installation.

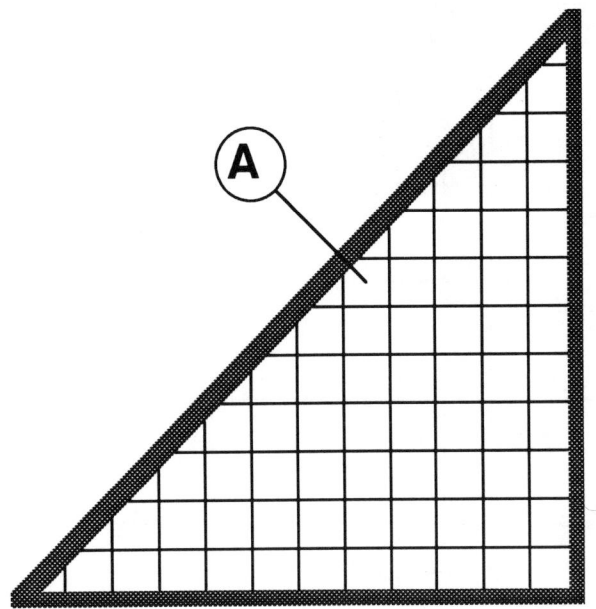
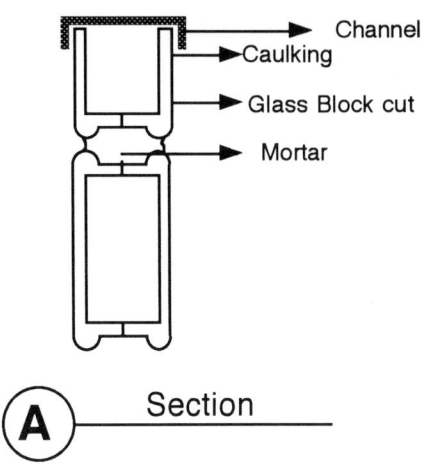

D.12: Custom perimeter chase panel and section

4. Association with other (dissimilar) materials.

(a) Accessories and small items:

- Vents are available in limited sizes. Most common are 8" x 8" (for one block opening), 8" x 16" (for two block opening), 16" x 24" (for 6 blocks opening). They can fit into a wall assembly or single inserts where ventilation is required or necessary.

- Tile, marble and granite can be installed to Glass block edges, vertically or horizontally. A wide variety of sizes will perfectly fit the open side of a free standing wall when matching end blocks are not available. And a bar or reception desk will be flattered by a varnished wood, granite, tile or marble counter top, provided that the appropriate support is set at panel assembling (see following Chapter "Installation").

- End Blocks, double end blocks, corner (90º angle and 45º angle) are available from many manufacturers but sometimes in limited sizes and patterns only. They certainly are handy, although very expensive, for multi directional panels, free standing walls, straight or curved and stepped applications. They can also be used for very precise shower panels where the hollow frame shower door may be securely fastened in between the grout joints (see next chapter "Installation"). Consult your supplier as to availability and prices.

- Small hooks, brackets and anchoring devices can be easily set at time of installation insuring a strong support and time saver further assembling, i.e to hold shelving, heavy picture frame or other anticipated decorative items.

(b) Windows and doors:

- Any aluminum or wood frame window can be permanently assembled in the middle or on the side or top of a panel. Architects will generally give proper details, and care should be especially taken with good quality elastic sealants and caulking applied to the perimeter of the contact of the two different materials.

- Door jambs cannot be (by Code) set in direct contact with the Glass Block, unless opening is properly "headed". A framing member will be used, wood or metal, as a standard "trimmer" and additional reinforcement should be provided for its attachments due to higher stress forces, movement and impact exposed to the end of the panel by frequent use conditions.

- Shower doors, however, may be directly anchored between Glass Blocks grout lines through the hollow frame light aluminum material of its components. It is usually done by bolting or screwing 1/4" device with plastic anchor inserted between the Glass Blocks at grout line which can be easily drilled with extreme caution so that the edge of the block does not crack.

(c) Artificial light:

-Whether directly or indirectly in contact, a dramatic effect will occur intentionally or unintentionally.

- Fiber optic: this recent, new revolutionary system of illumination can been adapted successfully to Glass Block panels. The method of installation is described more in detail in the next chapter. The main inconvenience for this procedure is certainly the high cost and tie consuming issue as well as a meticulous installation. It is easy to use it outside (on the surface) but the ultimate in interior Glass Block panels is really having the flexible fiber optic running through the wall, between the Glass Block courses at regular intervals, coming out unobtrusively at a lower end of the assembly to a concealed box where the light is sent through the fiber with an optional color change wheel device that will give up to five different tone-colors each few minutes in an endless spatial wave.

- Regular lighting can be installed such as a neon strip fixture under the counter top of a bar or reception desk. One single source at proximity of the panel, but not necessarily centered, would diffuse and spread uniformly through the surface. The natural light of a residential home at dusk will come through glass block windows and give a dramatic glow at night.

Office entrance
Curtom Building and Development
Glass Block Installers

Chapter 9

Installation

In previous chapters and on many occasions, I stress that good workmanship is the main key to attractive results in the use of glass blocks. As a building material, it is often considered as a delicate luxury item, and should be carefully treated during the course of construction.

Glass block is conducive to a multitude of personal tastes, architectural genres, and can make a home or office distinctive and distinguished by cleverly adapting the sizes, design and patterns.

The attractiveness of the glass block is compounded by the correct installation procedures which will give a result that pleases the eye because of its continuity and simplicity.

Glass Block installation may be divided into two distinctive sections and their related material as follows:

I. On-site assembly.

(a) Silicone installation
(b) Mortar installation
   1. Types
   2. Tools needed
   3. Material needed
   4. Preparation
   5. Step by step procedures
   6. Finishes and architectural details

II. Off-site assembly

(a) Structural applications
(b) Panels

I. On-site installation.

The typical piece-by-piece installation on site is the mostly used in commercial and residential applications, for vertical panels, such as window in fill. Various ways and techniques may be applied, depending on the use of the panel, its size and location but also Building Code requirements. Glass block installers must have a Masonry license C 29, by State License Board rules. However, many tile setters and glazing companies are progressively adding glass block installation specialty to their services offered. I personally suggest and insist that best results are provided by a skilled mason, in terms of durability, aesthetic and general guaranty. In this section, I intend to show to an homeowner handyman that with a mixed recipe of patience and belief, good and consistent result shall be obtained, if they follow the basics and instructions in this chapter. Convenient brochures of step by step procedures may be available from main manufacturers in the form of flyers or even video. They cover the most important steps through different methods but sometimes omitt that each situation may be different. On field professional experience will orderly classify.

Basic requirements will not affect if focal concentration is maintained.

The only two products that can bond Glass Blocks together in a proper manner are **mortar** and **silicone**. The only approved method by building officials is the mortar installation, and therefore highly suggested and preferred over silicone - with the exception of small quantities and surfaces at a decorative and cosmetic level, such as table stands, shelves supports, often applied in single or double row, bed platforms, where silicone bonding agent will be preferably used.

When dry, if it is a small amount such as the above described applications would need, the units can be free standing, thus removable and transportable, especially because of the weight reducing factor and density of silicone compared to its equivalent in mortar

(a) Silicone installation:

Advantages and inconvenience...

1. Maintenance: joints filled with silicone are exposed to dust, which is easily attracted and accumulated because of its sticky consistency and texture at touch. Mortar will retain particles but then easily wash off when quickly hosed down (see section Glass Block Maintenance, in chapter 5).

2. Strength: used on bigger walls and surfaces, reinforcement will not find their usual and necessary bedding thus application will not be comparable in terms of compression, impact and bond to its mortar equivalent when adding lime, cement and aggregate.

3. Approval: although there is no Code prohibiting its use, silicone application will not pass requirements and approval with Building officials on the job site. So, it should be limited to removable, free standing use and reduced square footage and/or quantity. Depending on conditions and exposition, in terms of security and safety, exterior panels should not exceed 15 to 20 square

feet, and avoided if possible, and interior panels should not exceed 60 to 80 square feet.

We must insist that it should be left to owner responsibility, judgment and liability. Remember we are dealing with a glazing material. Because of the void sealed in hollow unit compartments, and when one glass block is accidentally subject to breakage, pressure released tends to create a form of small explosion that can be dangerous and harmful because of shattering projections.

Basics and applications...

1. Usually, homeowners are seeking the look of clear uncolored silicone because of the natural-logical association with glass texture.

2. Installation is the other advantage because of small requirements of tool, speed and execution. The company "Pittsburgh-Corning" offers a kit called "Kwick-n-easy" in the form of a transparent plastic roll with a channel insert molded and designed to assemble glass block unit in a perfect fit holding them together while allowing the silicone to be easily applied into the joints created by this spacer type rubber material. The "kit" comes with:

- a plastic roll available in two dimensions to fit "standard" and "thin line" series, the only two thicknesses available for hollow glass blocks.
- a tube of silicone gun-type specially made for glass block bonding.
- a roll of plastic channel, which has a "snap" rail where the center line of the two halves units meet.

This kit may easily be replaced by other forms of temporary spacers and an extra strength silicone brand with good bonding and waterproofing properties. Self made spacers can be obtained with wood, plastic or cardboard pieces.

3. Because the translucence of glass is often desired when silicone is applied, block edge coating is usually scraped and cleaned off. Silicone components will here replace the edge coating primer type applied at manufacture. The most efficient way to remove that edge coating is to scrub it off with a strong razor blade, single edge type or good scraping tool (the reader must be aware that he or any other party cannot hold the author and the publisher responsible and/or liable for any claim when using such technique or practice as well as any other suggested throughout he course of this manual); then, polish it with steel wool to obtain smooth surface on all edges.

The main use of such application of silicone is for the fiber optic installation. Fiber optic is a new revolutionary system developed for lighting and communication fields. As to the glass block, the light is diffused trough the fiber flexible running in between the glass block courses in a regular serpentine pattern to equally distribute the light through he assembly. The edge of the fiber ends outside the panel into a terminal box (available with a color change wheel) producing a quite impressive result. The operation is costly and installation delicate and time consuming. The following shows the different steps for such silicone-fiber optic application:

Fiber optic - silicone installation:

First the units should have their edge coating cleaned off as described above. Most American manufacturers provide a white primer type of coating that will affect light diffusion. Others will use a transparent bonding agent type that may eventually be kept.

There are various methods to proceed. One is the use of plastic spin-off tab spacers available now at most glass block suppliers. The spin-off tab spacers are good for mortar installation and, if well used are a time saver and provide a clean and straight finish result. If not available, other self made spacers can be obtained with pieces of wood (wood shims) or cardboard, use temporarily until silicone is applied and panel is dry. Note that the fiber optic flexible "hose" or conduit, because of its regularity and thickness will make the best functional spacer for the purpose conveyed. Here are the basic step by step procedures:

Basic procedures for fiber optic installation:

As for all silicone installation, care should be made that panel size does not exceed a surface of approximately 80 square feet. Curved or straight wall, the procedure remains the same. All glass blocks are assumed to have their edge coating removed prior to install, as mentioned above, especially if white primer type is the agent used at manufacturing so that light transmission is not affected nor diminished.

1. The first row should be laid with mortar, plumbed and leveled, and let dry, to insure a sturdy base. Refer to mortar installation.

2. Apply a small strip of silicone (gun type system), just enough to tack the flexible fiber onto the top of glass block.

3. Start unrolling the flexible fiber in a straight line into the bed applied. Starting with the edge of fiber at the middle of the first glass block. If the terminal box is to be near the bottom, allow sufficient length to reach it. If the box is to be at the top or concealed into the ceiling for example, start with the end of the fiber and tape the extremity (about 1/2") with white duct tape to prevent extreme diffusion of ligth at cut end. One flexible fiber is enough to diffuse light or create the effect. But, despite the cost and since a limit size of fiber may be used because of the spacing required between the blocks, two flexible fibers, side to side, as shown on section A, will make a better natural spacer and light diffusion.

4. Lay the fiber as shown in sketch with bold line. Where the flexible fiber is to be folded to change course from horizontal to vertical, tape the fiber with white duct tape, just at the section where it will be bent at a 90º angle.

5. Leave the flexible fiber for the moment and apply a new strip of silicone, this time thick enough for the next glass block course to adhere to the first one. Do not spill over the edge of the glass block, stay approximately 1/2" away from the edges (that will be filled later with mortar).

D.14: Principal basic glass block wall with fiber optic

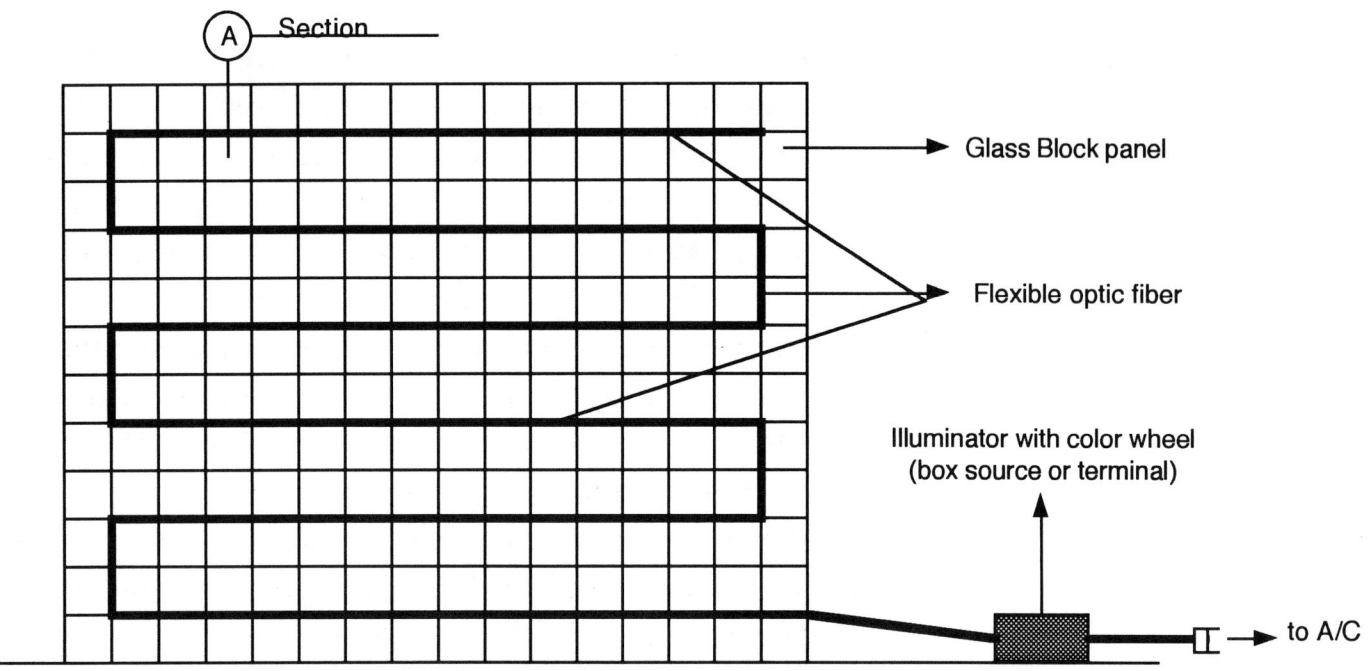

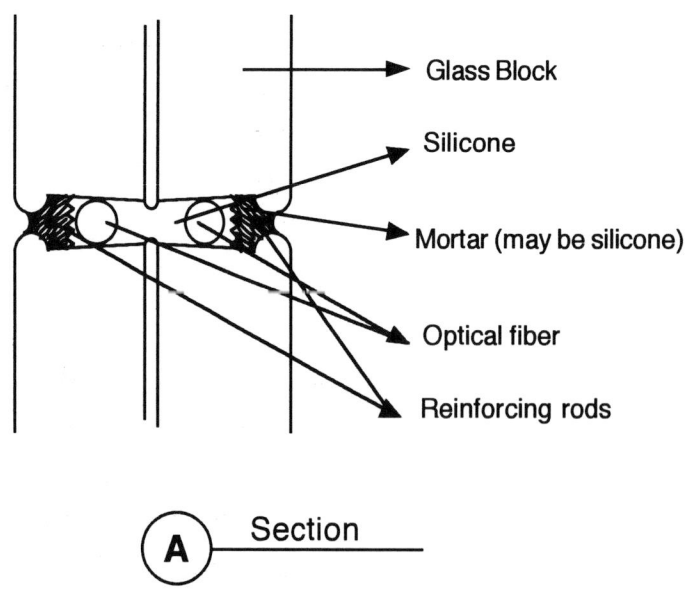

6. You may notice that one cartridge of the gun-type caulking material will not last you more than a couple of rows of a medium size wall 8 to 10 blocks wide. Now, install the plastic spacers (optional). Here, the spin-off tab plastic type is suggested. They have in fact a double function: they "lock" the flexible into position and receive the next glass block course while maintaining a temporary level and plumb to the work in progress.

7. Now, install the next row of glass blocks on top of the present course. You will notice as you go that the structure as it rises is not as stable and sturdy. Wait until it dries a little and carry on with the procedure. Make sure you are keeping the verticals leveled.

8. This next row should not receive the flexible fiber but instead the reinforcing rod as for standard installations. We still are using silicone to tack on the next row of glass blocks.

The goal of this procedure is to lay the entire wall of glass blocks with the spacers, silicone and fiber optic. Once done with the whole panel, you will notice that, after the silicone has dried out for a moment and because of the weight factor of the glass block assembly, the wall seems to be more stable and sturdy.

9. Now, carefully remove the "spin-off" tabs of the spacers (if used) by twisting them off with fingers or flat tool such as a trowel or a knife, or simply using the tab itself. Always use precaution so the whole wall does not get out of plumb.

10. You now have the choice of filling the joint

with mortar or silicone.

* With *silicone*, the strength will be resumed properly sturdy and the light will also be diffused through joints.
* With *mortar*, the structure will be stronger and the effect remains spectacular as the grout lines will show as a grid that will contrast with the translucency of the glass.

11. Apply mortar or silicone meticulously squeezing out the material into an approximate 1/2" void left as we were raising the panel.

12. Clean off and proceed for the cleaning as described for mortar installation (see next page).

This process may seem quite simple at execution and appears to be child's play but care and patience should be taken at all times as the plastic spacers sometimes cannot be relied on as to plumb and level of the whole assembly. Added to the very negligible size difference obtained at manufacturing during molding, you should not rely entirely on them as the level may come off plumb. That can be taken care of, using additional silicone during the assembly and little pieces of cardboard positioned temporarily until final grouting is done.

Silicone system is also used for grid assembly system. Some companies such as I.B.P (Innovative Building Product) in the U.S.A and Iperfan in Europe, provide a suitable and quality system. Finishes offered vary in wood, raw or varnished, and metal, polished brass and aluminum or bronze anodized. As to a step-by-step procedure, since assembly is resumed on-site, the manufacturer should provide with the delivery of its goods, a complete and appropriate instruction brochure or booklet. The basic rule is even simpler than the fiber optic method. Grids, whether used as a window or a skylight, are like cages ready to be assembled, where each opening has been conceived to receive a glass block unit and a small amount of silicone to lock it into position and keep it waterproof.

(b) Mortar installation:

This is probably the most delicate part of both this chapter and this book, since so many techniques may be used and applied. But materials, tools and sub-materials will not vary much. There are two basic forms of manual installation with mortar.

1. Types:

Perimeter chase installation which includes and also called **channel installation**. It may be required, because of type of building or code requirements, or simply chosen by the designer, architect or homeowner. It consists of a perimeter track where the glass block panel edges will be inserted into, usually (may vary with Codes) from 1/2" to 1", and usually made of galvanized steel, steel or masonry (brick or concrete blocks)

D.15a: Perimeter chase

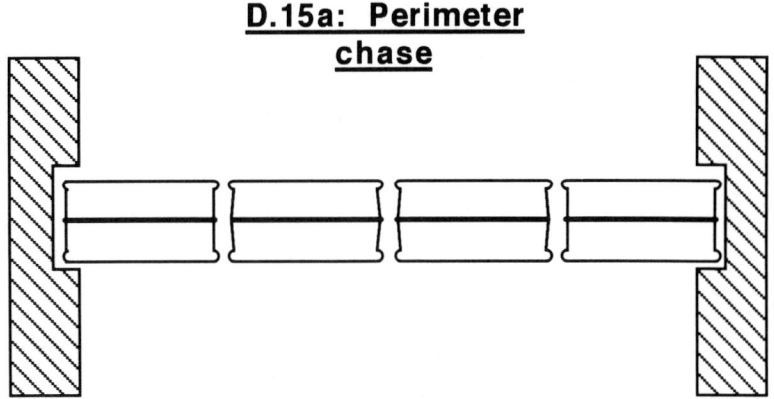

D.15b: Channel installation

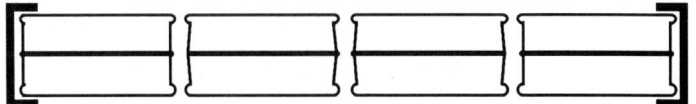

This method give the result of a picture frame type finish where the perimeter of the panel is diminished 1/2" to 1" all around. Channel may be apparent and/or painted, or covered with various finishing material (drywall, casing etc...) to match surrounding architecture.

Wall anchored construction. This method will be more widely used in residential applications, and where panels are inferior to the maximum sizes limit requirements, as seen in previous chapter related to Specifications.

D.15c: Wall anchored construction

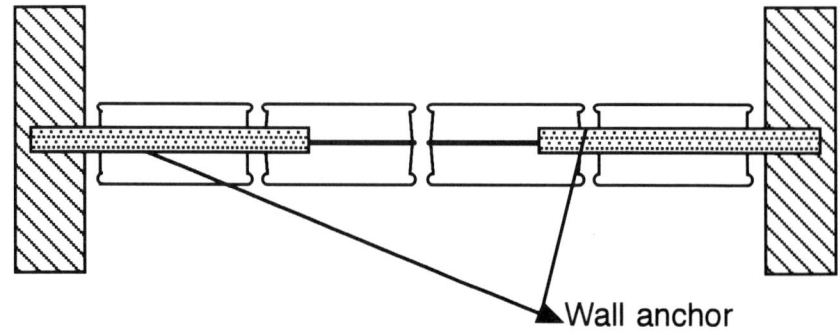

Wall anchor

page 128

Both of these methods are approved by the Building Codes and building officials. They are equivalent in terms of security, installation, durability, aesthetic and more generally, cost. Perimeter chase installation includes:

- structural steel (using "U', "I" and "H" steel beams.
- steel channels, usually galvanized "U" channel 14 to 16 gauge, depending on project requirements.
- masonry channels (brick or concrete blocks).

Channel or steel installations occur when exceeding panel size requirements (see table in previous chapter). For a minimum surface, the choice is a matter of taste, look and design, knowing that the insertion into the channel will have a 1/2" to 1" of the panel perimeter. One of the advantages of the channel installation is that, with the fact that glass block may be cut using a standard wet tile saw with diamond blade, more creative designs of panels may be obtained by customizing appropriate channels, as shown in chapter devoted to Designs and lay-out.

Glass block installation in construction, on-site and off-site assemblies, is to be performed, whether in new construction or remodeling, at <u>rough framing stage</u>. In other words, it is considered as a window or glazing component on the job site and must be installed at the same time. And except for interior partitions or cosmetic items, it should be set before drywall hanging and exterior covering (stucco, siding etc...). This is for the purpose of securing attachment to the structure or structural members, for waterproofing treatment and surrounding exterior and interior finishes.

Generally, free standing panels (one or two sides attached only) will only be installed at finish stage, but following the same step by step procedures.

2. Tools needed:

* trowel
* level (small 1" and 4" or longer)
* striking tool
* string or chalk line
* rubber mallet
* cutting pliers for reinforcing tie
* sponge (large size) and bucket for the cleaning
* wheelbarrow or batch to mix mortar
* steel wool for polishing (fine or medium)

Also, for preparation or attachment, according to various situations, basic tools may be needed:
* electric drill
* screw gun or screwdriver
* speed fastener (if anchoring to masonry)
* caulking gun and sealant cartridges

Make sure your tape measure is in good condition.

3. Material and sub-material required:

* glass blocks!!!!
* mortar or white plastic cement, silica sand and lime
* expansion foam
* reinforcing tie bars (or durowall)
* metal anchor (or wall anchor)
* spacers if you are using them
* waterproof additive to mortar if high exposition to moisture (shower, etc...)

* cold asphalt emulsion
* caulking
* channels (if chase installation)
* backer rods

Most of time, all of the above will be available at your local glass block or masonry supplier or construction yards. Masonry suppliers and large building discount surfaces tend now to provide a more complete selection of sub-materials used in the installation process. Before we start with the action, let's review and get familiar with the above described items.

(a) Mortar: two choices, premix or self-mix.

* Premix mortar can be bought at any glass blocks dealer and is time saver but slightly more costly than its equivalent. Usually it will require additional lime while working with it, as to consistency needed. For shower and high exposure to humidity and moisture, add water repellent or water proofing agent.

* If you mix your own mortar, you will need:
    - white plastic cement
    - silica sand, grade 30, 60 or higher
    - lime

The normal and most efficient mix is:

1 part cement + 1/2 part lime + 3 to 4 part sand

Go by shovels:
- 2 shovels cement
- 1 shovel lime
- 6 shovels silica sand

The higher the grade of silica sand, the finer is the mix obtained. If using waterproofing agent or water repellent, add to the mix according to manufacturer recommendations. It is best to prepare the batch as a first step before starting installation so it can rest for approximately 1/2 hour to a maximum of 2 hours. Do not add water after these two hours, mortar would lose its property.

The following table gives an approximate idea of quantities needed for the most common sizes of glass blocks mostly used. You should adjust and round off to the closest next size. Allowance should be made for special situations such as radius walls that will consume more volume at open joints. Also, small difference will be created in using either standard thickness (4" or 100 mm) and thin line (3" or 90 mm).

While mortar is widely preferred by glass block users because bright whiteness increases the refracted light through the pane. Polymer, as component of white cement, provides strength and repels water.

D.16: Mortar quantities

	6" x 6"	8" x 8"	12" x 12"
Premix 60 lbs	30	25	15
Premix 90 lbs	40	32	20
Mortar*	80	70	40

* by cement volume, 1 bag of cement = 90 lbs

In accordance with ASTM C 1142, Standard Specifications for Ready Mix Mortar for Unit Masonry, and C 270, Standard Specifications for Unit Masonry.

Table No. 24-A -- Mortar Proportions for Unit Masonry

Mortar	Type	Portland cement or blended cement[1]	Proportions by volume (cementitious materials)						Hydrated lime or lime putty[1]	Aggregate measured in a damp, loose condition
			Masonry cement[2]			Mortar cement[3]				
			M	S	N	M	S	N		
Cement-lime	M	1	—	—	—	—	—	—	1/4	
	S	1	—	—	—	—	—	—	over 1/4 to 1/2	
	N	1	—	—	—	—	—	—	over 1/2 to 1 1/4	
	O	1	—	—	—	—	—	—	over 1 1/4 to 2 1/2	
Mortar cement	M	1	—	—	—	—	—	1	—	Not less than 2 1/4 and not more than 3 times the sum of separate volumes of cementitious materials.
	M	—	—	—	—	1	—	—	—	
	S	1/2	—	—	—	—	—	1	—	
	S	—	—	—	—	—	1	—	—	
	N	—	—	—	—	—	—	1	—	
Masonry cement	M	1	—	—	1	—	—	—	—	
	M	—	1	—	—	—	—	—	—	
	S	1/2	—	—	1	—	—	—	—	
	S	—	—	1	—	—	—	—	—	
	N	—	—	—	1	—	—	—	—	
	O	—	—	—	1	—	—	—	—	

[1] When plastic cement is used in lieu of portland cement, hydrated lime or putty may be added, but not in excess of one tenth the volume of cement
[2] Masonry cement conforming to the requirements of U.B.C Standard No. 24-16
[3] Mortar cement conforming to the requirements of U.B.C Standard No. 24-19

In glass block masonry, Type N will be used for interior and type S for exterior. In all cases, refer to your project specifications and requirements and/or manufacturer recommendations.

References for mortar:

* Masonry cement ASTM C 91, white cement for high strength use.
* Portland cement ASTM C 150, Type I, white and waterproof.
* Hydrated lime ASTM C 207, Type S, High Calcium, pressure hydrated dolomite with minimum of 92% of completed hydrated active ingredients.
* Sand ASTM C 144 for aggregate for masonry. Clean, silica type sand or white quartzite, all grain size (100%) to pass a #12 sieve. No iron compound for solar reflective (as it would damage for oxide coating). Accelerators and antifreeze should not be used.

The mortar should be mixed to a stiff but workable consistency and may be re-tempered (add water) unless used 1 1/2 hour after mixing> However it should be drier than regular masonry mortar since glass blocks are non-absorbent.

Waterproofing may be added, even if using waterproofing plastic white cement, especially for exterior window, shower or other highly exposed installations for dampness.

Type of waterproofers permissible:
(a)-Metallic Stearate Type, Sonneborn Contech (Stereatic acid)
Model Hydracid powder by Masterbuilders Co.
Model Amicron Mortarproofing.

(b)-Latex Type (liquid) by Laticrete International (#8150 Model Laticrete, high strength resistant mortar and fast bonding agent.

Note: mortar color may be added at anytime and treated as for concrete or stucco application.

(b) Expansion strip:

They are made of dense glass fiber batt or polyethylene plastic white foam. According to glass block thickness used, strip will be either 3" or 4" wide. Thickness is 1/4" to 3/8" and it is sold by rolls or strips of 24" long. It is provided by main manufacturers and suppliers.

It is used and required along jambs (vertical sides) and atop (head) of panels. It provides for contraction and expansion of mortared glass block panels and structure set and stress (such as building soil movement, new building settling, earthquake...).

(c) Reinforcing bars:

They look like a double wire meshed "railroad" tie type. Made of 2 parallel 9 gauge rods, 1 5/8" to 2" apart, once again depending on the thickness of glass blocks used, and tied by cross rods of the same gauge butt welded and spaced at 8" (approved dimension), but can be also purchased with 16" on center cross ties. The final material is hot dipped galvanized after welding to 1.25 oz. (of zinc) per square foot (1.25 oz./sq.ft or 380 gr/sq.M).

Section in accordance with ASTM A 153, class B2 and A 82, cold drown steel wire (hard tempered) ladder type.

This material is installed horizontally between glass

block courses (required to be at 24" on center) and provides for continuous reinforcement to ensure structurally sound glass block masonry.

(d) Panel anchor or wall anchor or metal anchor:

20 gauge flat steel strip (9 mm), comes in only length of 24", 1 3/4" wide (44 mm), punched with three rows of elongated notches, alternating in a staggered pattern, hot dipped galvanized or electroplated after perforation, to resist corrosion. They are used to attach the glass block to the structure or channel, and installed and sealed in between two rows of glass units, embedded in mortar and placed where reinforcing bar occur (requirements at 24" on center horizontally), to the sides and top of panels.

They are flexible enough to allow bending to the desired location. Holes are to receive anchoring or fasteners (screws, bolts 1/4", nails or welding) depending on type of structural member and requirements.

Panel anchors provide for the resistance of panel to the structure and lateral forces and has been tested at about 54 p.s.f.

(e) Spacers:

Metal spacers: galvanized, 24 gauge, flexible aluminum, perforated with circular holes to allow mortar penetration and setting. They come 36" long and 2" wide, and will fit both glass block thicknesses. They provide firm support for horizontal lining of courses, preventing undesired sagging. Horizontal joint will be maintained at 1/4" to 3/8". they can be easily bent and broken to be used for radius walls.

Plastic spacers: made of white plastic polyethylene, by various manufacturers and with different designs.

* spin-off tabs: the most popular and efficient but the most costly. Legs may be cut to form a T or a L (see diagram) as the installation develops. They may be used for curved walls but will not provide the same accuracy. However, they should not be fully relied upon, as the whole panel may lose its plumbed level.

Available in the two American Standard thickness, 3 1/8" and 3 7/8". They will not fit metric size blocks perfectly but may be used. After raising panel (see installation procedures), you will need re-grouting after removing the tabs. The main advantage is that those spacers give the most perfect and regular grid and joints thickness.

* accu-speed: (by Meyer Equity, Inc.), made of rigid plastic. Connector type designed for straight walls and curved walls. They will fit any size of blocks, American Standard size or Metric sizes. Walls need not re-grouting as with the spin-off tabs, but care should be made and level maintained, each courses when raising panel. Their perforations will allow them to be fastened or connected to frame or structure.

* reusable plastic spacer: the central plastic tie may be replaced and four prongs tabs of both sides will be then reused. Will fit any sizes and thickness, American and Metric system

* "veri-tru": same basic as the spin-off tab, but tab is replaced by flexible supporting legs. More reliable and efficient for curved walls. Manipulation will be delicate and more time consuming but worth while.

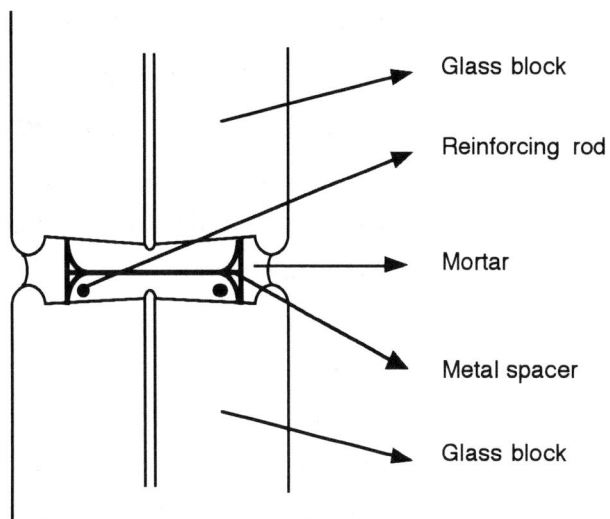

D.17: Cut view of metal spacer position

(f) Caulking and sealants:

Use acrylic, silicone, urethane. Need to be non staining, waterproof. This material is to be in accordance with ASTM C 920, Grade NS, Class 25. One part polysulfide or polyethurane and specified by C.S.I, Section 07900, Joints Sealers.

Color may be selected. Usually the gun type is the most efficient as it is applied at perimeter only as an isolant from other materials in contact with the structure.

(g) Backer rods:

Usually described as packing on drawings and project manuals and requirements. It is mostly used for chase installation to fill space between glass block and channel metal ledge at perimeter of panel deep enough (1/2" in general) so sealant can be applied. Sold in rolls of 3/8" diameter, made of polyethurane foam neoprene, oakum or equal.

(h) Asphalt emulsion:

Required at sills for any exterior installations and when in contact with moisture or humidity. Cold application type and brushed on the sill surface for the width of the glass block to be set.

Water based type are the mostly used. Most often specified item is Karnak 100 920 by Karnak Chemical Corporation (1-800-526-4236.

(i) Channels:

14 to 18 gauge aluminum channels or galvanized steel. Comes in both thickness of glass blocks for thin line and standard sizes. Available at most suppliers but best to be ordered from your local sheet metal shop for good savings.

4. Preparation:

Visualizing the work as if it were already done is the best suggestion anyone can get at this point, before taking the next step. Examine the perimeter area of the entire opening where the panel is to be installed. This will prevent surprises for eventual upcoming difficulties or unexpected obstacles. Check the surrounding structure and review the following check-up list:

(a) Glass blocks are non-load bearing. Despite their high compressive strength ratio, they are designed only to support themselves and their components elements of installation, and should not be considered to support any member of the construction. However, it can be said that the panel, once properly installed will "help" reinforcing the surrounding structure.

(b) No additional or dedicated base, support or foundation is required if assembly is less than the limit size requirements in length or height. If exceeding those dimensions, area of support will require proper engineering and foundation or bases sizes calculated.

(c) Usually, glass block installation, in new construction and remodeling, should occur at rough framing stage, before any wall, ceiling or floor covering, when exterior or interior. Shower enclosures have to be installed after rough framing and hot mop laying. In certain cases, if using marble or granite slabs, it is preferable to wait until the wall, pan and ceiling are covered. For interior partition, dividers and other similar decorative items, (usually small surfaces), they may be installed after wall covering (drywall, tile, marble, hardwood floors...). Never install glass blocks directly over carpet. Use the proper isolant material of preparation as shown on table at following page.

(d) All sides (head, jambs and sill) where glass blocks to be applied, must be solid, to receive required fasteners (nails, bolts, screws) and permit secured attachment of masonry panel anchors (for panel anchor installation) or to secure channels (for perimeter chase construction). For example, do not start nor attempt laying glass blocks where drywall, plywood or other non solid covering is not properly backed (reinforced) by a stud (metal or wood) or concrete. In case of a free-standing wall (bar, reception desk etc.) which means having one, two or three sides attached to the structure, the same rule will apply. When a free-standing wall has only one side for attachment (floor attachment) and especially if the panel is flat and/or exceeds 4'0" (1.32 meter) you may use a rigid flat bar sealed between the vertical rows near the free standing end, and permanently sealed into the floor, under the first horizontal course.

When building curved walls and cornered panels with 45º or 90º corner blocks,, then natural stability will result to reinforce the free-standing wall.

(e) Check your sizes! If new construction or remodeling is in progress, opening will be built to fit the desired size of glass block. But if you are trying to replace an existing window or filling an empty existing opening, you might have to do some alteration to the surrounding structure, add some wood filler, drywall, tile or maybe compose your panel with different sizes as discussed in chapter 8. If I may advise the skilled mason, installer or homeowner, do not start installation before you confirm the opening dimensions and proper size is obtained. For enclosed openings and allowance between members (jamb to jamb and floor to ceiling), the best rule of thumb for is as follows:

> **Glass block nominal size** X **Number of glass blocks** + 1"

i.e.: regardless of thickness, if you want to install 8" x 8" blocks, 10 units wide and five units high, you will need a rough opening of:

8"(size of block)x10 pieces = 80" + 1" = 81" for width
8"(size of block)x 5 pieces = 40" + 1" = 41" for height

The nominal is used because it already includes 1/4" for grout joint required for installation.

> **Nominal size = Actual size + Grout line or thickness**

See table for most common sizes of glass blocks available in metric and standard sizes. For metric sizes, adjustment should be made. American Building Code required 1/4" to 3/8" for grout joint, horizontally and vertically. European Standard uses 30 mm or 1" of mortar. You may also use the following rule:

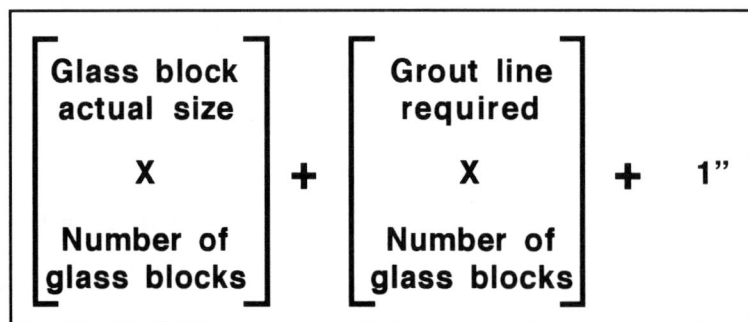

page 142

Basically, this allowance is needed where installation occurs at rough framing stage for three reasons:

1. Expansion foam at jambs and head is required.

2. Finish material used at surrounding.

3. Level adjustment allowance. Rough framing members and construction may not be perfectly leveled and plumbed and glass block proper installation has minimal percentage of error. Therefore, perimeter must be able to be adjusted in anticipation of covering material, which makes it an additional reason to be installed at that stage.

The following diagram is to help visualize the panel to be installed and anticipate surrounding covering materials around the perimeter when work has been completed (shown with dotted line). You should be aware of the thickness used by each of the surrounding finish materials and that will be used at wall covering stage:

i.e.: drywall maybe 1/2" or 5/8"
    tile maybe 1/4" or 1/2"+ mortar set 1/2"
    granite/marble will take 1 1/4" + float 3/4"

As mentioned above, rough framing member may not be perfectly plumbed and panel must be in following diagram, we have exaggerated a header and a sill unplumbed and definitely not parallel. Although the situation should be corrected before installation commences (if more than error allowance standard), this example will illustrate our intention.

D.19: Finishes anticipation

Ceiling (expansion required)
- drywall (1/2" to 5/8" etc...)
- tile (1/4" to 1/2")
- granite (3/4" to 1 1/4")
- suspended ceiling

Jambs (expansion required)
- drywall or float (showers)
- tile
- granite or marble
- stucco
- bricks
etc...

Floor or sill (asphalt emulsion required)
- hardwood
- slate, pavers, stone ...
- linoleum
- carpet
- tile, granite, marble ...
etc...

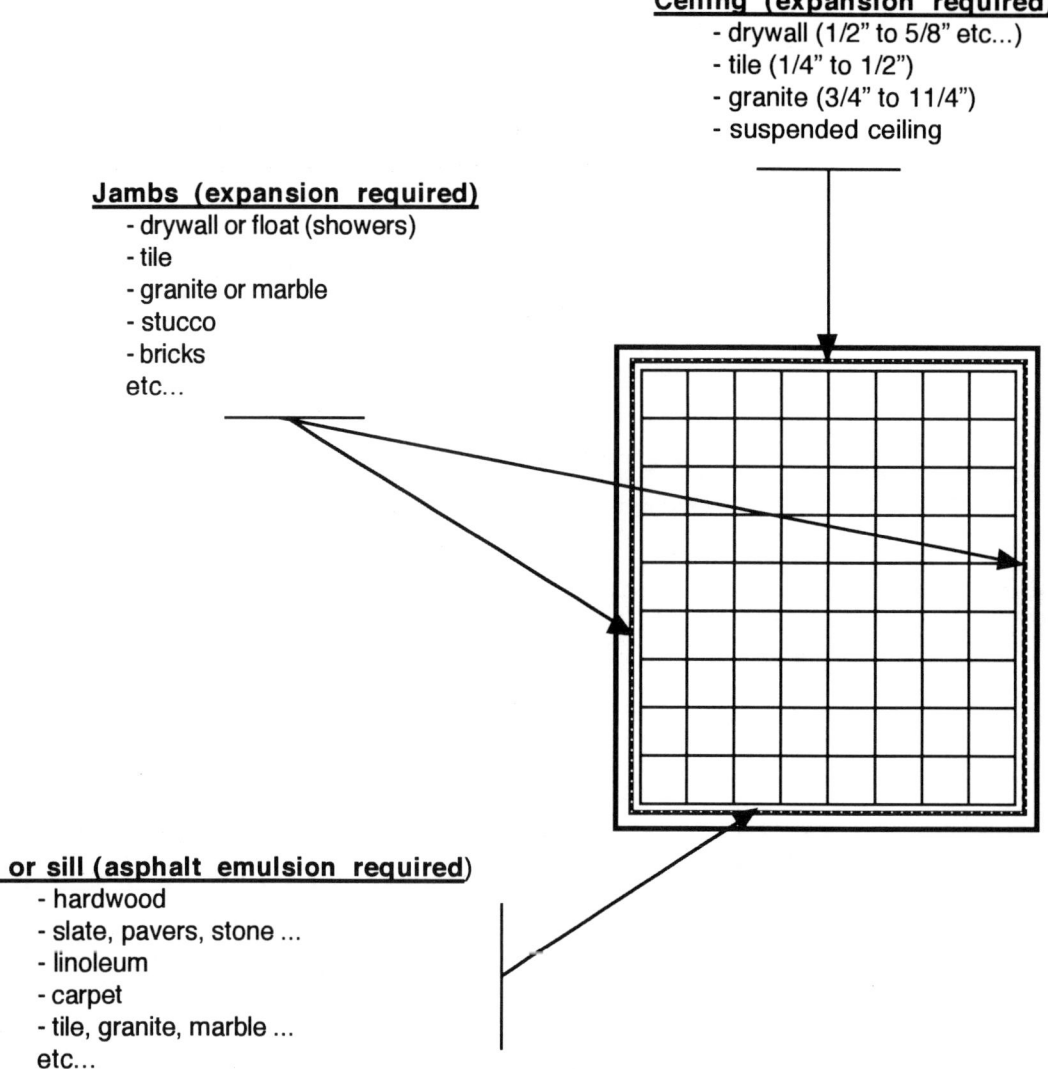

D.20: Unfavorable job site conditions
(exaggerated)

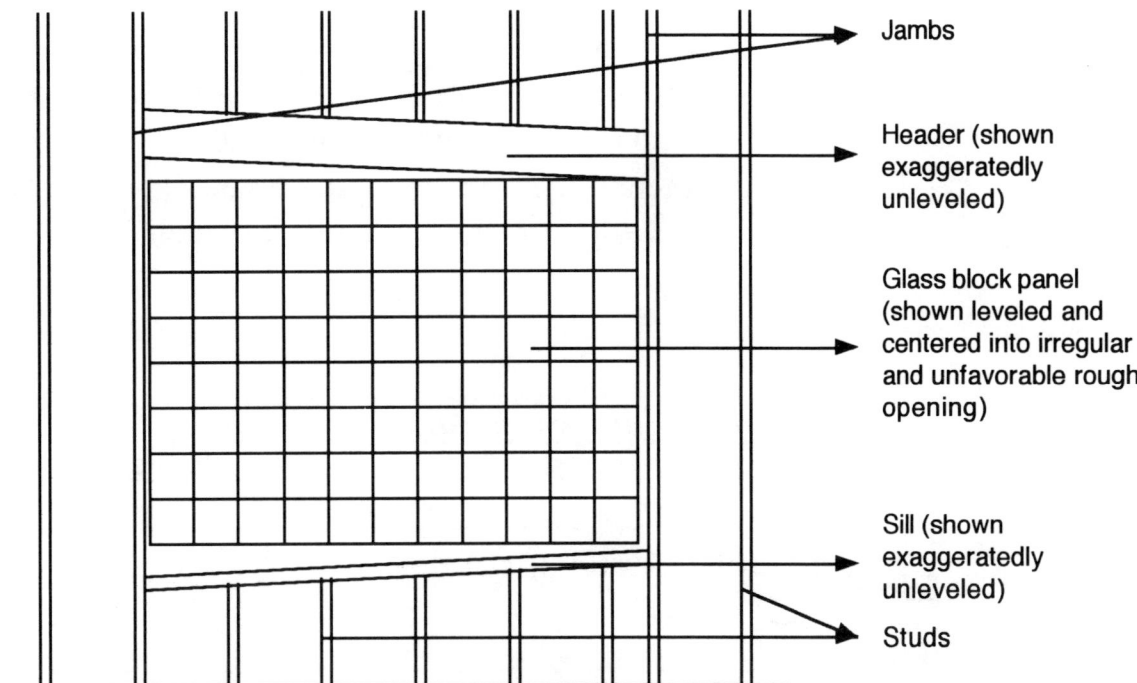

(f) Finally, surface should be treated before laying our first bed of mortar and row of glass block. The following table (D.21) will show surface preparation for most common surface situations and appropriate material to receive glass block panel. Whatever the case may be, you will need one or more of the following preparation materials

- asphalt emulsion
- primer
- sealer
- flashing paper or felt paper
- channel (optional)
- expansion foam (required)

You may also refer to figure D.21, about finishing around the glass block. Architectural details provided in that chapter refer to a number of various situations.

Additional situations to following diagram:

* Tile, marble, granite: (bathroom, kitchen, interior panels) You may install directly on tile, marble or granite which are water resistant. Use only expansion foam at jambs, and head. Pre-drill material with appropriate drilling bit and plastic anchoring device to secure channel or metal anchor before installation of expansion foam.

D.21: Most common surfaces preparation required before laying mortar and glass blocks

	Concrete and bricks	Wood		Metal
		Rough (exterior)	Finish (interior)	
Jambs	1. Asphalt emulsion 2. Expansion foam or 1. Asphalt emulsion 2. Channel 3. Expansion foam	1. Flashing paper 2. Expansion foam or 1. Flashing paper 2. Channel 3. Expansion foam	1. Primer or sealer 2. Expansion foam or 1. Channel 2. Expansion foam	1. Primer 2. Asphalt emulsion 3. Expansion foam or 1. Primer 2. Asphalt emulsion 3. Channel 4. Expansion foam
Sill	1. Asphalt emulsion 2. Channel (optional)	1. Flashing paper 2. Asphalt emulsion or 1. Asphalt emulsion 2. Channel	1. Primer or sealer 2. Asphalt emulsion 3. Channel (optional)	1. Primer 2. Asphalt emulsion or 1. Primer 2. Asphalt emulsion 3. Channel
Head	1. Asphalt emulsion 2. Expansion foam or 1. Asphalt emulsion 2. Channel 3. Expansion foam	1. Flashing paper 2. Expansion foam or 1. Flashing paper 2. Channel 3. Expansion foam	1. Primer or sealer 2. Expansion foam or 1. Primer or sealer 2. Channel 3. Expansion foam	1. Primer 2. Expansion foam or 1. Primer 2. Channel 3. Expansion foam

* Drywall (interior panels only). When installing directly over drywall or sheet rock, make sure it is backed with metal or wood stud behind surface (drywall, wood paneling or other) receiving the glass block to secure channel and/or metal anchor. Also prime two coats where glass block is to be installed because of property of absorption of drywall. Chemicals or mortar (silica and lime) may slightly damage the texture. Therefore, paint or wallpaper should be applied ***after*** glass block installation.

* Hardwood floor base (interior panel only). Do not start installation on raw wood. Seal first area where glass units are to be laid upon with flashing paper (excess paper can be trimmed off after panel is installed) or wood sealer for the width of glass block to be used. In this case, most of time, one or two two-by-four wood studs will be secured at base of panel so that wall base molding may be continually installed throughout the entire room.

* Carpet: never install glass blocks over carpet directly. Cut carpet and padding if any for width of glass block to be used or remove carpet. Remove "tacking" wood. Add necessary amount of mortar to obtain proper height so first course is not obstructed. After installation, adjust carpet around the base. Reinstallation of carpet may be required.

The following diagrams show the first phase when in rough framing situation and the first step for preparation at jambs (sides), head and sills. As previously discussed, jambs and head will receive the same preparation (no mortar).

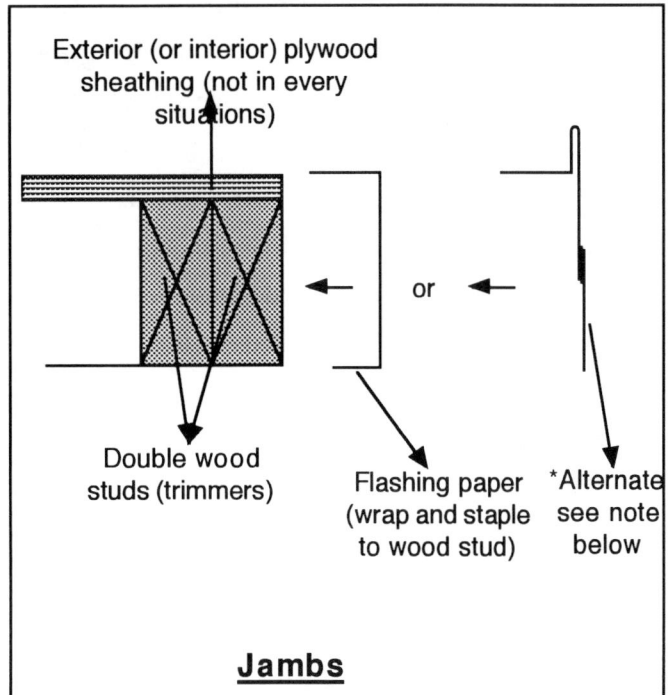

Jambs

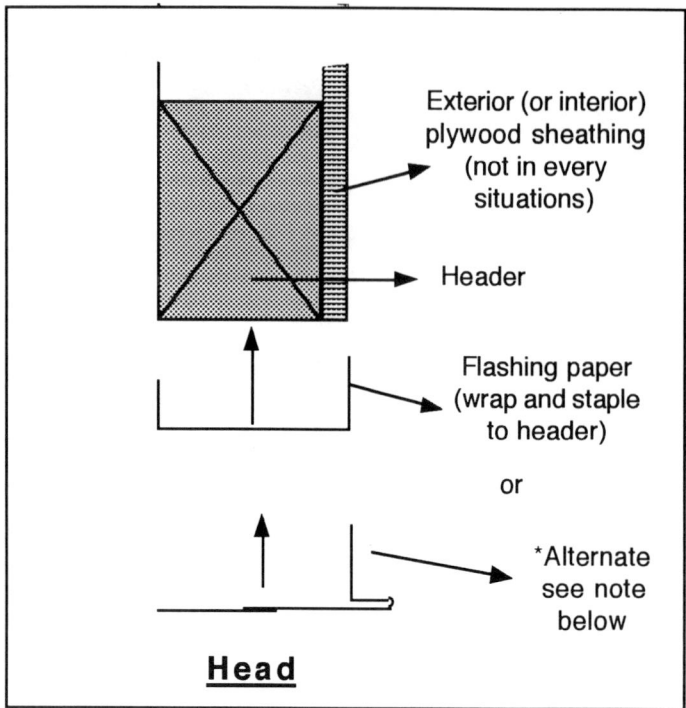

Head

*Note: flashing paper may be replaced for a more costly but more secure 20 gauge galvanized flashing that will provide better waterproofing for the structure. Below a enlarged detail of cut section of metal flashing. Also, note that, at a further step, stucco bead (or milcore) will not be needed. When installing, nail or screw to structure perimeter and seal all connections and nail or screw heads.

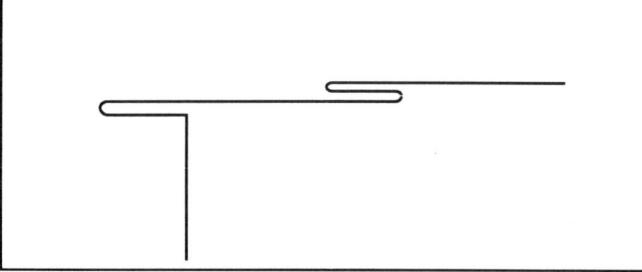

Note: Thickness of stud (3 1/2") + Thickness of plywood sheathing (3/8") = Thickness of glass block standard (3 7/8"), therefore glass block can be easily and equally centered into 2 x 4 framing

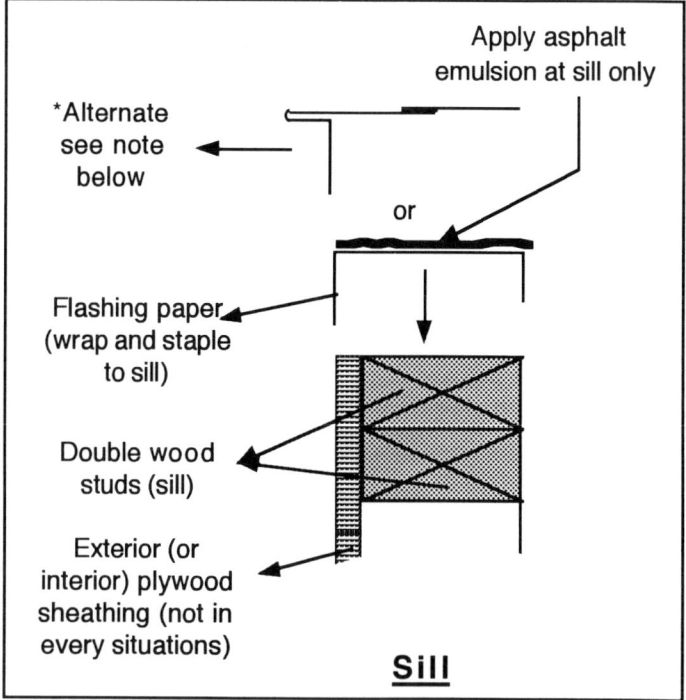

Sill

D-18: Phase 1: Install flashing paper or galvanized metal flashing.

5. Step by step procedure:

Standard wood framing installation, most popular and efficient condition, will be shown. Other conditions use similar method but apply different preparation as described in table D.21.

(a) Install flashing paper at perimeter, sill, jambs and header members. Use a standard stapler, hammer stapler or other similar.

(b) Spread a full bed of mortar to the sill (or base) for the full width of the block to be used. If first course is lengthy you may want to proceed by section of 4' to 5', depending how fast you will install the units, so the mortar does not dry. You may alter the amount of mortar at sill accordingly with the finish material edge line anticipated that will contact the lower course of glass block, such as drywall, wood casing, tile, carpet etc.. (see preparation) so the first grout line may or may not be visible. You want to have at least a minimum of 3/4" to 1" before setting the block on the mortar bed.

Optional: drop into the mortar bed a metal spacer guide (see accessories and material needed) to help you with alignment and reinforce at the same time the mortar base. Press it so it is fully covered by the mortar. Try to lay the mortar evenly as shown:

D.22: Mortar at sill

Note: do not furrow mortar at sill or courses

Install (stick or staple) a strip of expansion foam at each jamb or side for the height of the first glass block only. Cut expansion (strip or roll) accordingly to glass block size used, to allow metal anchor (reinforcement) to be set against the jamb, under the following strip of expansion foam. See next picture

(c) Install a glass block on each side (or jamb), dry, without any mortar. It could happen that you may need to apply mortar on side in contact with the expansion strip. You should just place the glass block and tack it. It should just stick to the mortar if correct consistency is obtained at mix. Tap it slightly with back rubber of your trowel or hand, enough to hold it in place until the remaining ones are in place. Then check the following three levels; vertical, horizontal and lateral.

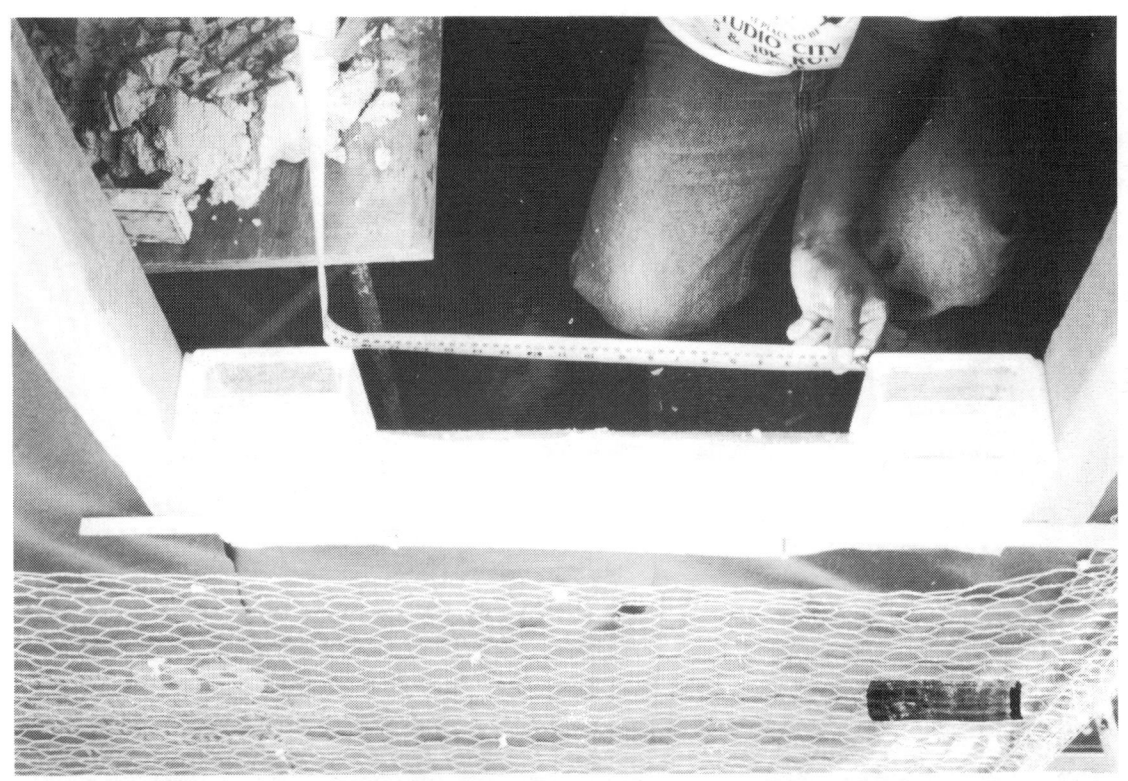

(d) Measure distance between left and right block, which operation is more delicate when building curved walls. It should fit the remaining number of glass blocks to be installed at first course plus one grout line allowance (1/4"). If correct dimension not obtained, move slowly left and right units so course is balanced between desired finished vertical supports. Example: if 10 glass blocks of 8" x 8" American Standard size remained to be installed at first course, totaling then 12 units, you should have 10 x 8" = 8"1/4" between the left and right blocks. It is a good idea and almost imperative that you should lay the first course dry without any mortar at sill as a lay-out to obtain the proper setting of first course.

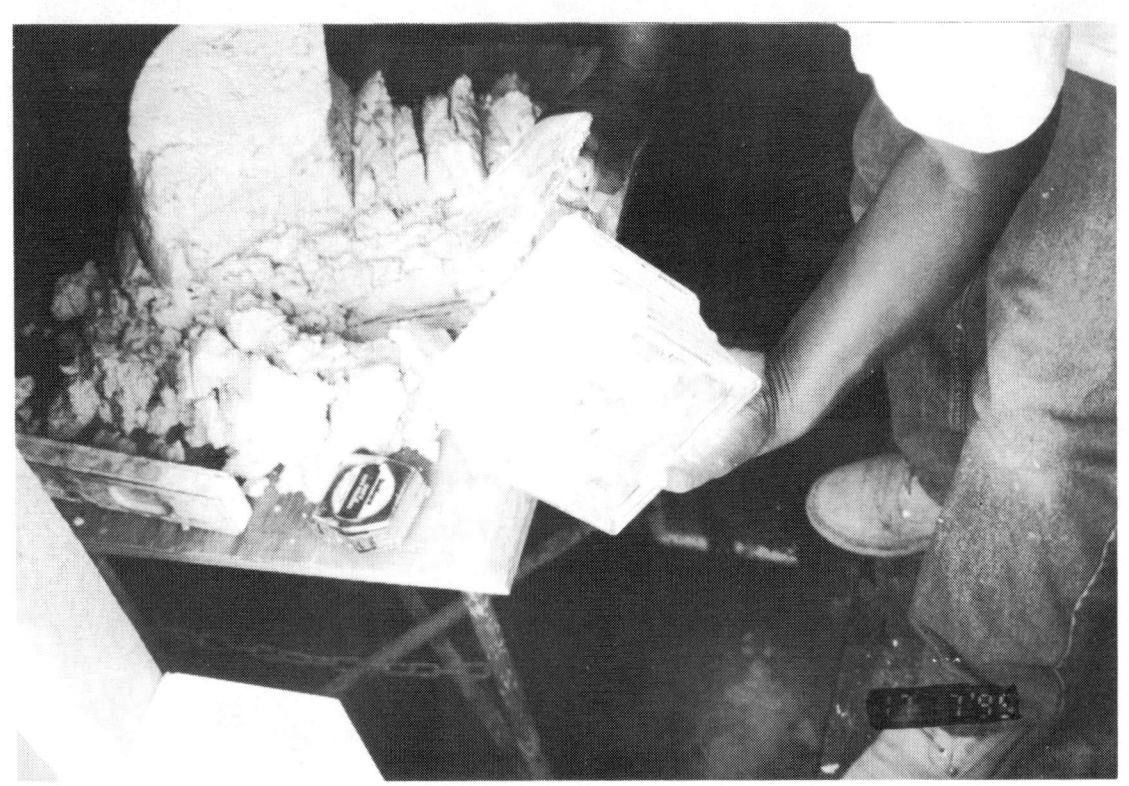

(e) Install now the remaining blocks as follows: "butter" each block on one side only. Watch for pattern (or design) to be aligned if any. Apply approximately a 1" spread of mortar evenly, on the full side surface of the block.

Gently tap the block in place against the previous installed and align it vertically and horizontally.

You should work on both side simultaneously and alternate one block on each side so that the last block of the course is centered on the course. The last block of the course should be mortared on both opposite side.

* Check the three levels
* Do not over mortar the sill and the block, so you don't have to push the block too hard into place thus lose the level.

(f) A good and safe technique or feature is to install now a string line at the desired top of first course from left to right (side to side). It should be tied at same distance from base or floor with allowance of mortar for finished covering materials and assuming that base or sill is leveled so the string line touches the top of glass block's first course Optional: you may pull a second string line at back of first course to secure horizontal and vertical levels.

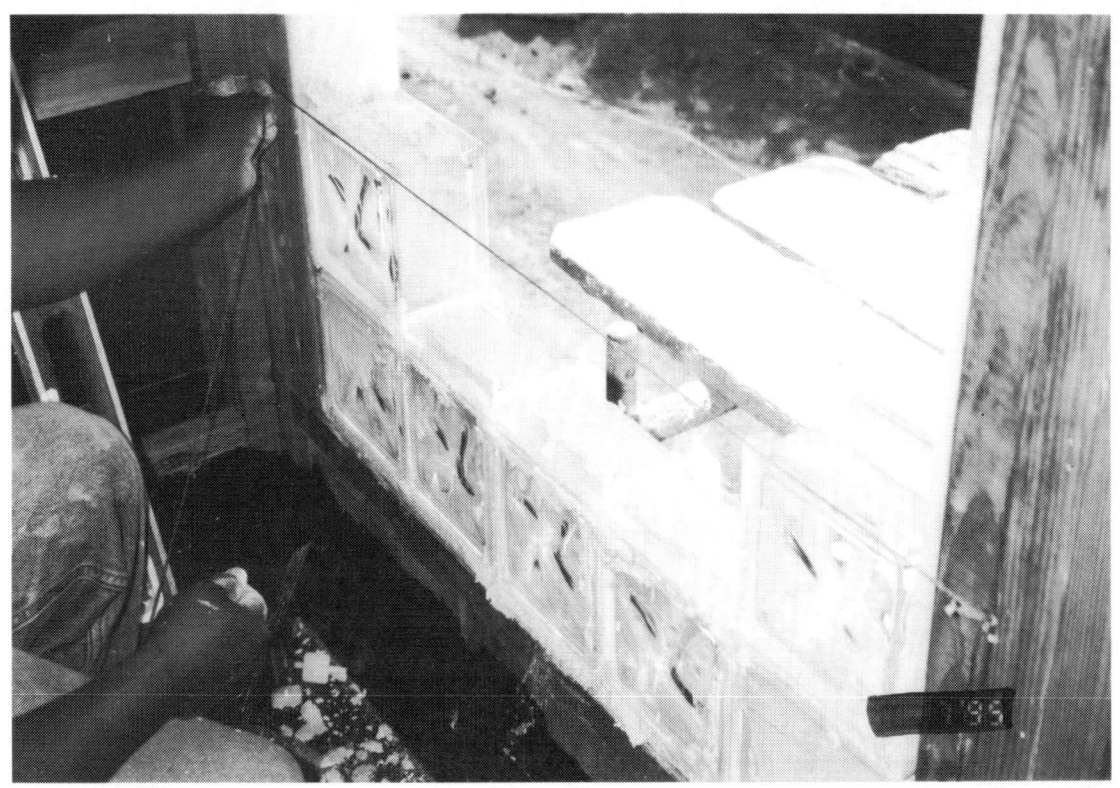

* Let dry a few minutes before correcting another time all three levels..

* Your first course and levels are the key of your entire panel, so spend time on it and secure levels.

* Remove then the string line(s) if installed.

* Fill top and side joints if voids exist.

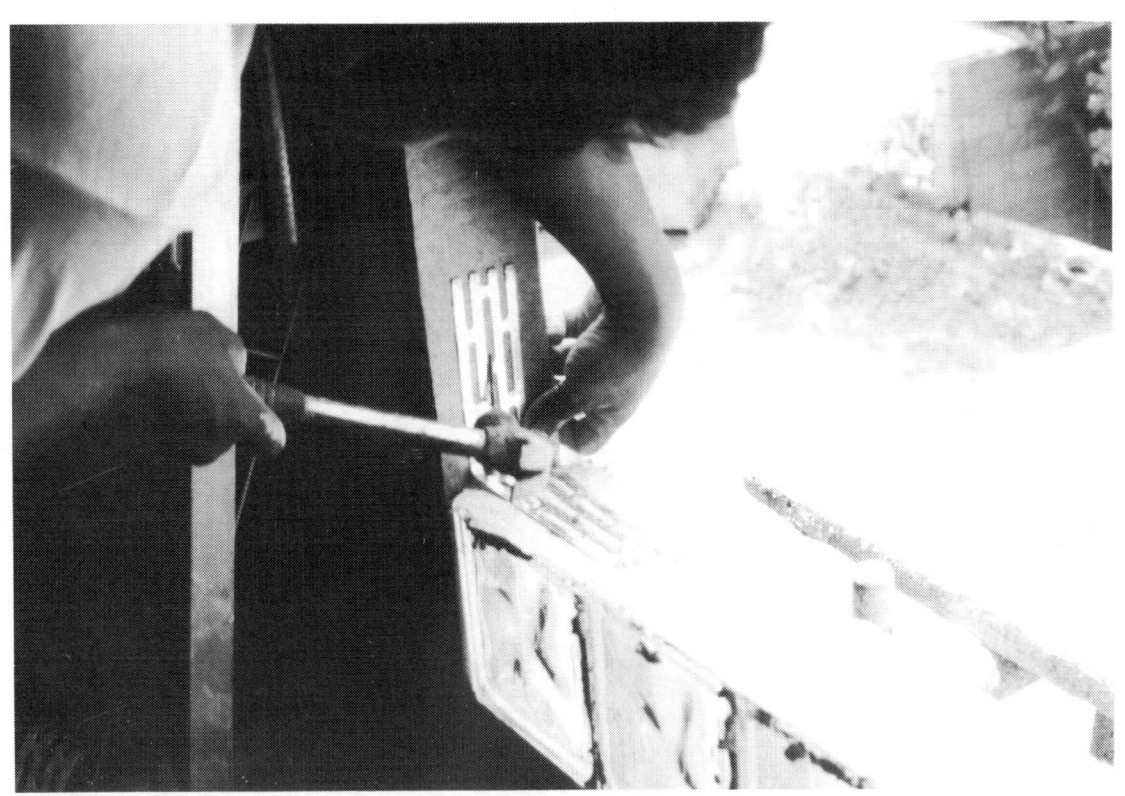

(g) Bend a metal anchor at a 90º angle and secure it to the sides (or jambs) as follows with appropriate devices fasteners (nails, bolts or screws), depending which material is used in structure (wood studs, metal studs etc...) and immediately install a 2' strip of expansion foam that will cover it. The reason you want to have 2' of expansion foam in place is that reinforcement only happens every 2'0 on center horizontally (see Code and Specifications).Therefore this operation (g) next happens at the fourth course.

The top of the metal anchor should rest atop of the first course of blocks. A slight amount of mortar should be applied between the first block and the metal anchor so the metal anchor is firmly embedded between first and second course.

* Reinforcing rods are installed where metal anchor occurs.
* Reinforcing rods and metal anchors are required:
    1. on top of the first row.
    2. every 24" thereafter or every three rows of 8"
         every four rows of 6"
         every two rows of 12"
    3. before last course.
    4. on top of every opening if existing.

In any case, refer to specifications when available or architects and/or project special requirements.

Cut rod to desired length. If more than one section is necessary, overlapping of reinforcing rod should extend 6" at least.
When reinforcing rod has been cut, remove it and

apply another bed of mortar, evenly and approximately 1/2" to 3/4" on top of the first course, as shown on D.22, which should be stiff enough so the next course does not sink in. Place then and press in the reinforcing rod across, so it is totally embedded into the mortar. The reinforcing rod should start 1" from the side or jamb and overlap the metal anchor at least 1'.

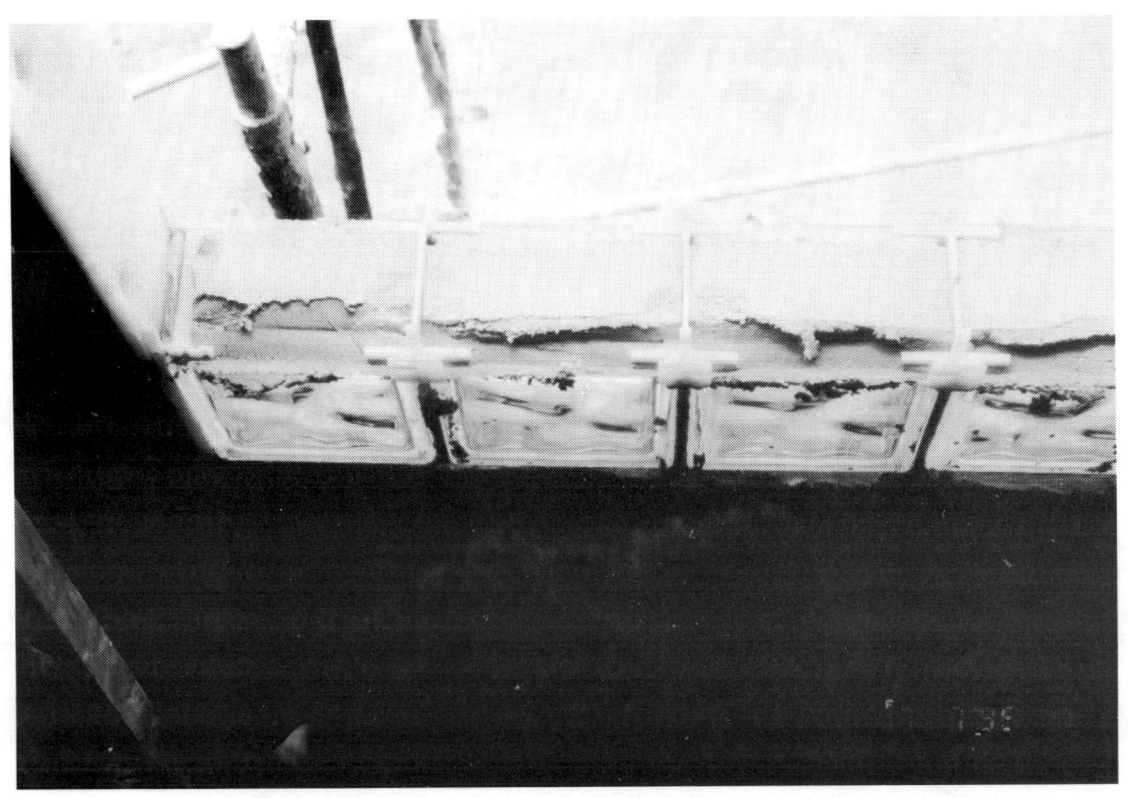

(h) Optional: install now spacers, metal or plastic (see accessories section), if using any. For plastic spacers, the most popular and easy to use, spin tabs off with spatula or similar flat tool, when using it at corners. If using metal spacers, press onto the mortar after laying as described above.

(i) Proceed thereon as for first course. Install left and right blocks first, and remaining thereafter. Always check your three levels. See (d) to (f). Continue with proceeding until last course is laid. When panel completed and all glass blocks installed, you may let dry about 15 to 20 minutes. Remember to always check your **3 levels** every course, if you are using spacers or not, to prevent error and movement.

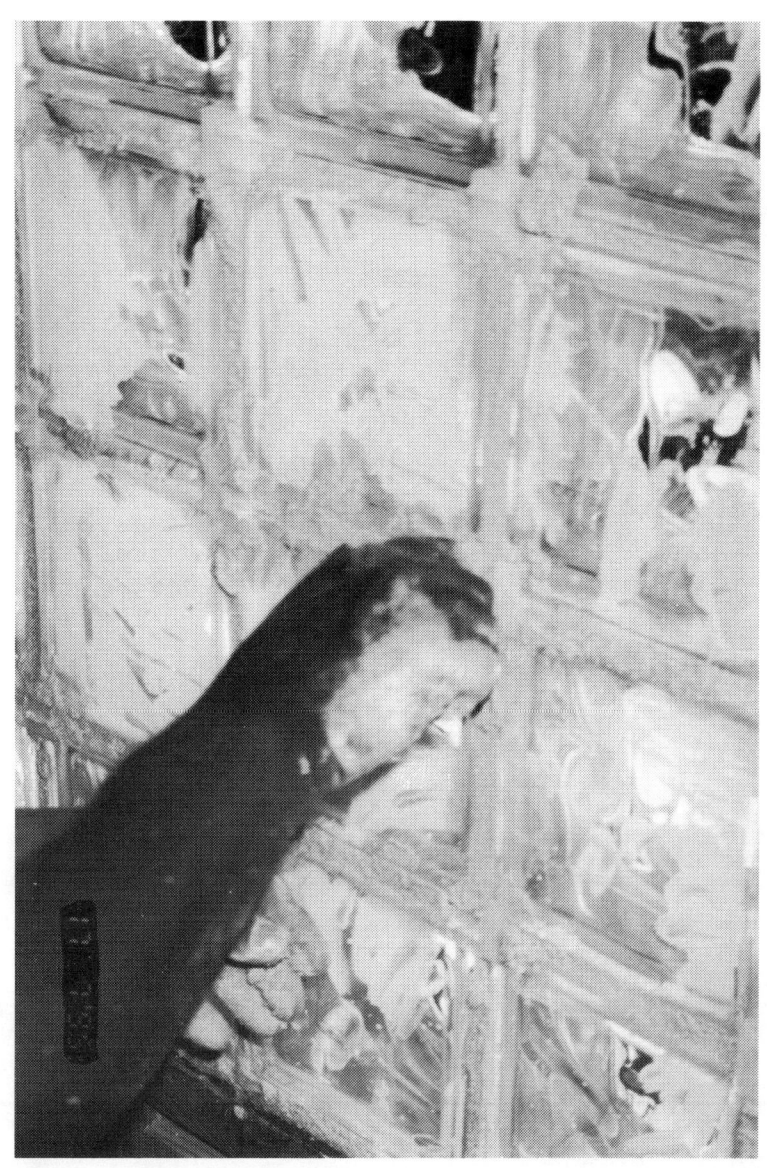

(j) If using plastic spacer, spin off tabs now.

(k) Remove excess grout off joints and add grout where more is needed with your hand, applying the mortar with the hand in a rolling motion, rather than using tool or trowel, which could scratch or chip the glass.

* Rubber gloves should be used at all times during installation, due to corrosive properties of chemicals used in mortar mix and lime.

(l) You now need a bucket of fresh water and a couple of clean sponges. Wipe off the two sides of panel with sponge, floating and rinsing it frequently until all excess of mortar has been removed and only a think film is visible when drying at ambient room temperature. Give caution not to give too much pressure to keep the panel leveled and plumbed. It is a good idea to check the levels as you clean and strike the joints. Let dry 15 to 20 minutes until mortar comes to a paste consistency.

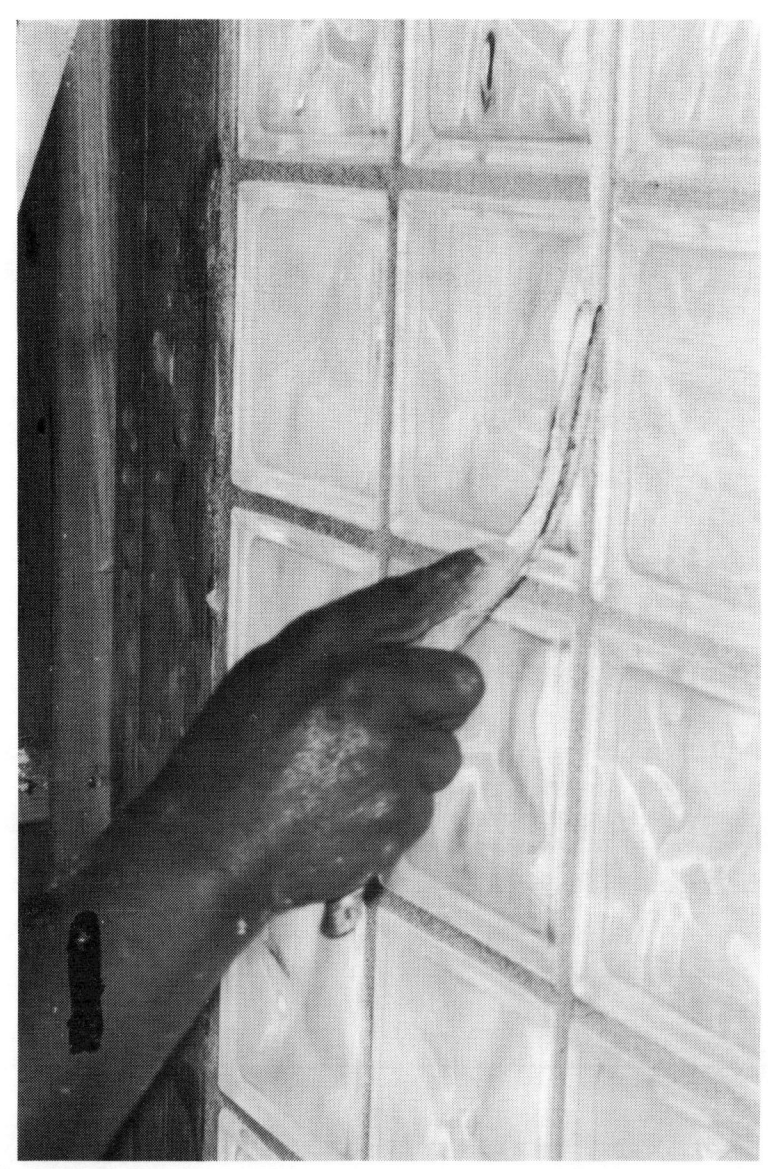

(m) Strike all joints with appropriate tool, carefully to avoid chipping, horizontally then vertically. This procedure provide the mortar compaction necessary for a better waterproofing and smooth finish of grout lines. Again, let dry 15 to 20 minutes.

(n) Wipe off again the panel sides to remove excess mortar from striking, until light film appears. Let dry for a moment. Depending whether on weather conditions, provide artificial heat if cold or damp area to accelerate steps if desired.

Using a fine steel wool, gently brush off both sides of the panel to remove final film of dry grout as a final step to polish your glass block panel, giving it a final shine.

Your panel is now complete. Even if it still does not feel totally sturdy, make sure your level is maintained and wait until completely dry.

When panel is dry and has cured in approximately 24 hours, depending on the ambient temperature and weather. Sealant should be applied around exterior and interior perimeters, between the panel edges and surrounding material. Use caulking gun type and industrial grade of sealant.

II. Off-site assembly:

For this section, I choose to refer to "Circle Redmont", the main company in U.S.A that is standing in this field and with whom I had the pleasure of working several times with, on the West Coast and even in Kuwait. They have constantly supported and have helped me over the years and with regards to this book will perfectly achieve the content of this section.

Off-site assemblies include both vertical and horizontal applications; commonly called "panels" or "grid systems", they may be divided into two types:

(a) Non structural applications: glass block panels, such as windows, mostly for horizontal purpose, and using hollow units, are assembled into a removable or permanent frame (according to design sought), wood or metal, following the step by step procedures of mortar installation, as previously treated. After curing, each unit is rated and delivered to the job site, where they are installed into the structure just like window units. If preformed at manufacture, the surrounding wood or metal will offer systems of attachment to secure the unit, such as metal ties, that may be screwed, nailed or bolted to the adjacent framing or masonry. If no frame is provided with panels, the opening to receive it, will be adequately prepared so masonry or metal can lock in securely the whole assembly.

Advantages are that when small units in reduced quantity are needed, labor may be cut back. Size of each panels should never exceed an approximate 25 square feet, because of the weight produced by mortar and glass block combination, and the maneuverability during hauling and installation. This system however remains delicate and is rarely used for curved walls or windows due to error that could be produced in building radius, unless they are properly shown and detailed on the appropriate shop drawing before assembly.

An alternative to "non-structural" panels is the "grid system" (See silicone application). Various manufacturers, such and Iperfan or IBP, offer metallic or wood frame with different finishes, pre sized and built to receive most common size of block, such as 6" x 6" or 8" or 8". Each block is inserted into own opening and will be locked into single compartment and secure with application of silicone around edges and interior and exterior perimeter.

(b) Structural applications: a "structural" panel is a combination of glass block and metal or concrete and is used for horizontal and vertical applications using preferably paver units but occasionally hollow units. They may be divided into two categories: metal and concrete, where each unit is individually sealed into a single compartment, similarly to the grid system, creating a structural combination with the steel or reinforced concrete . Various applications are generated: decks, bridges, stairs and stairwells, floors, skylights, ceilings and entire wall systems.

Again, because of massive weight produced by such combination, division and fabrication of each panel to be assembled must be carefully calculated. Structural applications and analysis for such reinforced glass block panels are similar to the one used for reinforced concrete and structural metal. Additional compression naturally generated by combination, will not, however, be structurally effective in engineer analysis. A pitch of 1/4" per foot will be required for skylight or exterior deck or floor. When several panels are assembled together, the appropriate span may be structurally supported by two opposite sides only. Fewer companies specialize in such manufacturing where quality and perfection are necessary and must be very precise, liability and esthetical result will be prominent into the project considered.

I have had the pleasure and privilege to work years with Circle Redmont®, based in Florida. Their name and reputation has expanded and prospered in this unique field. All Circle Redmont® innovative advances in materials and procedures are truly producing "Products Engineered to Last a Lifetime". Founder Fred Saunders has these comments to make.

"All the variables associated with conventional glass block lay up procedures document that it is virtually impossible to guarantee the performance of this type of installation.

Circle Redmont®
Panels shipped and crated ready for assembly
University of Kuwait City, Kuwait
Z.X Construction / Glass Block Installers

"On the other hand, Circle Redmont's warranted assemblies completely eliminate this hazard.

"Circle Redmont® Prefabricated Glass Block Panel Systems were developed to further enhance the use of glass block as well as to eliminate the problems typically associated with conventional glass block lay up, namely quality of installation, time to erect, mess, repairability or maintenance, and overall long term performance.

"Circle Redmont® is the recognized leader in the engineering and fabrication of prefabricated monolithic glass block panels incorporating various types of grids and blocks to meet specific design, load and performance criteria.

"Circle Redmont® Prefabricated "Solarwhite" Hollow Glass Blocks Panels incorporate extruded aluminum grid framework. Special Circle Redmont® engineered extruded aluminum shapes are cut, notched, punched and welded to exacting standards to form a matrix into which the hollow glass blocks will be inserted. The finished grids are then placed on flat and true lay up areas and the glass blocks are inserted into the completed exacted openings. Our proprietary waterproof 6 part thermal fill is then poured between the glass block then vibrated to fill the entire cavity and allowed to cure. After curing, the units are prepared to receive either a Circle Redmont® finish grout or silicone joint seal. This unique fabrication process produces a structural, waterproof hollow glass block panel of unequaled quality. Since our proprietary assembly is capable of controlling any thermal dynamic loading and is unaffected by temperature or

Circle Redmont®
Panels are hauled and carefully set in place
University of Kuwait City, Kuwait
Z.X Construction / Glass Block Installers

Circle Redmont®
University of Kuwait City, Kuwait
Z.X Construction / Glass Block Installers

moisture, it can be used in any climate and, since the panels are structural, they are suitable for a variety of uses. Additionally, since each glass block is set into an individual cell opening, any damage to one block does not affect any other block making replacement of any block a simple procedure capable of being performed by inexperienced personnel. Conventionally laid up block cannot compare with the many advantages of our prefabricated systems.

"Circle Redmont® Engineered, Prefabricated "91 R" Glass Block Panels are fabricated incorporating a welded steel framework and solid glass block pavers to any loading requirements. Circle Redmont engineered steel shapes are factory jig cut and welded to exacting Circle Redmont® standards to provide a dimensionally true and warp free grid. Typically, all steel grids are sandblasted to full white metal and receive our Circle Redmont® standard typical five mil epoxy prime paint finish with exposed surfaces receiving two coats or two part urethane finish when factory finish is requested.

"Finish frames are set on straight and level support beams. Circle Redmont® standard waterproof glass block bedding is then inserted in the glass paver support framework. The glass pavers are then jig set into the frames onto the bedding exactly centered within the opening providing accurate spacing of the pavers both vertically and horizontally. Circle Redmont® multi blended waterproof grout type material is then installed using Circle Redmont® unique process to ensure perfect density and bonding of our blended materials. After an initial cure process the panel

Circle Redmont® Vaulted panels
University of Kuwait City, Kuwait
Z.X Construction / Glass Block Installers

is either finish grouted with Circle Redmont® finish waterproof grout or silicone sealant. This multi step process assures the highest possible quality and proven product performance. Flat, curved, angled or cambered units are available within this system.

"Circle Redmont® "71 R" Prefabricated Concrete and Solid Glass Paver Panels are state of the art structures, engineered and fabricated to provide a waterproof assembly capable of supporting a wide variety of structural loadings. Circle Redmont® special concrete molds have a unique computer designed shape with all intersections radiused to specific dimensions which produce a stress free performance enhancing panel. Circle Redmont's two parts molds are arranged on specially engineered pour platforms to exacting dimensional tolerances. The engineered steel cage structure, previously fabricated to our exacting standards, are placed within the mold and secured to ensure accurate position. Next, Circle Redmont® developed and blended standard 5000 lb minimum concrete mix is prepared to near zero slump and placed within the form. Our special high frequency vibration causes this stiff concrete mix to readily flow completely, eliminating any chance of voids or air pockets. After cure, the concrete grid work is air ejected from the mold and placed in a special finish cure area.

"Circle Redmont® special "71 R" waterproof bedding is next placed within the cell openings and the glass pavers are installed. Our specially blended waterproof grout type mix is introduced at this point to complete the assembly. Circle Redmont® 71 R Prefabricated Concrete Panels are available in standard and all custom concrete colors and finishes and have demonstrated their reliability and performance over the past quarter century."

Bibliography

* *Masonry Design and Detailing*, Christine Beall
* *Masons & Builders Library*, Volume II, by Louis M.Dezettel, revised by Tom Philbin, 1986.
* *Handbook of Architectural Acoustics and Noise Control*, Pettinger TPR, 1988
* *Traditional Details*, 1932 to 1950, A.I.A
* *Time Saver Standard for Architecture and Design Data*, John Hancock, Collerator, 1982
* *Construction Materials, Types, Uses and Application*, 2nd edition, Coleb Harnbostel
* *Masonry Estimating*, Reynold V. Kolkoski, Craftsman 1988
* *Construction Materials for Interior Design*, William Pupp, Arnold Fredman, 1989
* *Reinforcing Steel and Masonry*, M. I. of A, 1991
* *Architects Details Library*, Fred A. Still, 1990
* *Masonry Design Manual*, M. I. A. C., 1979
* *Architectural Handbook of Construction*, David Kent Ballast, 1990

References and Technical Assistance

The end of the manual contains brochures courteously provided by various company of manufacturers and/or suppliers most dedicated to the glass block market.

Also, please refer to Chapter 3 about manufacturers and their contact. Further edition of the manual will include up dated material.

Glossary

Terms and expressions used throughout the manual and in glass block construction and manipulation in general:

Control joint: joint space created within a glass unit panels to allow dynamic and/or thermal movement to occur at the joint and not cause any cracking within the panel assembly.

Expansion joint: joint space created between glass unit panels and adjacent construction to allow dynamic and/or thermal movement to occur at the joint and not cause structural damage to the panel assembly.

Expansion strip: compressible and expandable filler material used at expansion joints and at a glass unit panel perimeter.

Flashing: sheet metal or sheet membrane placed under the glass unit panel to direct moisture from behind the panel to the exterior.

Hollow glass units: glass block units with a hollow core, with or without pattern and or design.

Joint filler: compressible material placed to control expansion joints. This material is compressible and expandable to fill the joint space under joint movement conditions.

Mortar: cementitious mix of cement, sand, lime and water used in the installation of of glass masonry units.

Panel anchors: metal strap used for attachment of panel to surrounding structure.

Panel reinforcement: reinforcement tie bar used at horizontal joint.

Perimeter chase: structural frame or masonry surrounding perimeter of glass unit panel.

Running bond: laying glass units to a horizontal pattern by overlaying each masonry unit to 1/2 coverage of the unit below.

Stack bond: laying glass units to a horizontal pattern by stacking each unit directly over the unit below.

Solid glass unit: glass block units with a solid glass core.

Index

A...
Accessories.. 112
Anchor...136
Applications... 31
Asphalt emulsion.. 139

B...
Backer rod... 139
Basic Building Code.. 70
Bibliography.. 176

C...
Caulking.. 138
Channel details..91, 92
Channel installation..128
Channels...91, 112, 139
Compressive strength..69
Conversion table.. 73
Corner block.. 33
Corning-Reubens..8, 9
Curved walls.. 74

D...
Design...98, 101, 103

E...
Edge coating... 121
End block... 24
Energy transmission... 37
Expansion foam, strip...135
Exposure..99, 100
Exterior details..85, 86, 87

page 180

F...
Fiber insert... 41
Fiber optic... 34, 114, 121, 122
Finishes... 82, 144
Flashing (metal)... 148
Flashing (paper)... 144
Fusion.. 19

G...
Gerrix-Glassteine©... 26
Glass block making.. 5
Glossary.. 178

H...
History.. 7

I...
I.D.G.. 28
Installation... 116
Interior details.. 87 88, 89, 90, 91
Iperfan©... 26

J...
Joint thickness... 74

L...
La Maison De Verre... 10, 11
Light transmission.. 38, 42
Load bearing.. 69

M...
Maintenance.. 48
Manufacturers... 23
Manufacturing... 17
Maximum size limit for panels.............................. 70, 71
Metal anchor.. 34, 136
Minimum radius... 75, 76
Module... 142
Moisture... 47
Mortar... 131, 132, 133
Mortar additives.. 134
Mortar installation.. 127
Multiple panels... 93

N...
N.E.G... 27
National Building Code.. 70

O...
Off site assembly... 165
On-site installation... 117
Oversized panels.. 95, 96
Owens... 9

P...
Pavers... 172
Physical properties.. 36, 72
Pittsburgh Corning©................................. 8, 11, 12, 13, 24

Preparation..140, 146
Privacy...40, 46

R...
Rule of thumb...142

S...
Saint-Gobain©...27
Sealants...138
Security..44
Selection..93
Silica sand...17
Silicone installation..119
Sizes (most common sizes).......................................77
Solaris©..25
Sound transmission...43
Spacer..120
Spacers..136, 137, 138
Standard Building Code..70
Standard Specifications.......................................51, 54
Step by step installation..149
Structural applications..166

T...
Thermal resistance...39
Thermal transmission..72
Tools...130

U...
Uniform Building Code..52
Uses 31

W...
Wall anchor...136
Weck©..25
Wind resistance..44

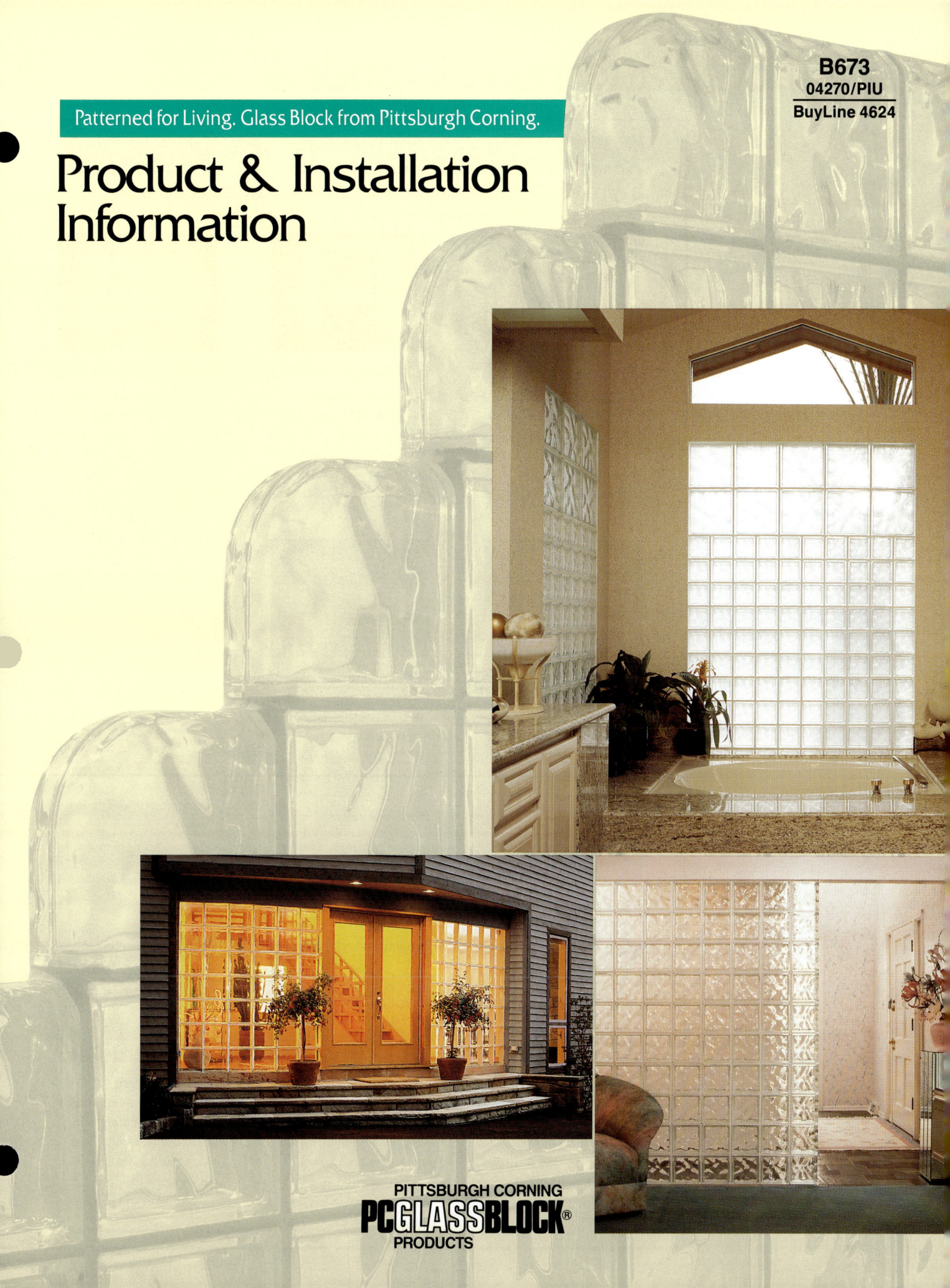

Products, Patterns & Options

A jewel-like variety of sizes, shapes, patterns, thicknesses and types of Pittsburgh Corning PC GlassBlock® Products is waiting to bring your design ideas to luminous reality. Here are square, rectangular, hollow, solid, reflective, corner, angle, finishing and paver blocks to suit every design application you can envision.

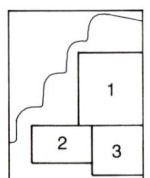

ON THE COVER:
1. Indian Ridge Country Club
   Architect: McLarand Vasquez
   & Partners
   DECORA® Pattern with
   LX Fibrous Glass Insert
   Photographer: Arthur Coleman
2. Private Residence
   Location: Fox Chapel, PA
   VUE® Pattern
   Photographer: Tom Cwener
3. Private Residence
   Location: Pittsburgh, PA
   Designer: By builder
   DECORA® Pattern with
   EndBlock™ Unit
   Photographer: Robert Henshaw-Suder

REGULAR SERIES

The REGULAR and PREMIERE Series offers the widest variety of sizes, shapes and patterns for the ultimate in design flexibility.

ARGUS® Pattern
Rounded flutes at right angles on each face diffuse light while allowing maximum light transmission and a medium degree of privacy.

VUE® Pattern
Faces are smooth and undistorted to transmit the most light and allow ultimate visibility. This is your best choice for passive solar collection and visual clarity.

DECORA® Pattern
With its trademark wavy undulations, this pattern provides maximum light transmission with subtle visual distortion. The nondirectional faces make installation quick.

ESSEX® AA Pattern
The fine grid design of the closely spaced ridges in this pattern offers uniform light transmission of a moderate degree with the maximum degree of privacy.

TEXTRA™ Pattern
Depending on the light and angle of view, the face pattern alternates among grid, basket-weave and lattice patterns. This exciting new pattern features a directional design.

THINLINE™ SERIES

The THINLINE™ Series is specifically designed for prefabricated panels of limited size and applications where weight is a consideration.

CIRRUS™ Pattern
This pattern combines the wavy undulations of the DECORA® pattern on interior block faces with a stippled texture on the exterior faces to further reduce transparency without sacrificing light transmission.

DECORA® Pattern
With its trademark wavy undulations, this pattern provides maximum light transmission with subtle visual distortion. The nondirectional faces makes installation quick.

DELPHI® Pattern
This raised diamond design lends a prismatic effect to the light it transmits. You won't find a more effective combination of light transmission and privacy.

04270/PIU
BuyLine 4624

PREMIERE SERIES

EndBlock™ Finishing Units
The rounded, finished surface on one edge of these blocks makes them virtually disappear when used vertically or horizontally on the edges of panels, walls or dividers.

HEDRON® I Corner Block
The hexagonal shape of this corner block makes it perfect for turning 90-degree corners in projects such as partition walls. It is available in two sizes in the DECORA® pattern.

TRIDRON 45° Block® Units
The unique shape of this block lets you create everything from 45-degree angles to full circles. It's available in the eight-inch size in both DECORA® and VUE® patterns.

Encurve™ Finishing Unit
With arched, soft edges to round out your design options or finish panels. Use with 8"x 8" EndBlock™ Finishing Units for a stepped panel.

Pittsburgh Corning Glass Block Patterns and Sizes

PATTERNS & SHAPES	SIZES*				
	6"x 6" Nominal (5¾" Actual)	8"x 8" Nominal (7¾" Actual)	12"x 12" Nominal (11¾" Actual)	4"x 8" Nominal (3¾"x 7¾" Actual)	6"x 8" Nominal (5¾"x 7¾" Actual)
REGULAR SERIES (3⅞" thick)					
ARGUS®	x	x	x		
DECORA®	x	x	x	x	x
ESSEX® AA		x			
TEXTRA™		x			
VUE®	x	x	x	x	x
THINLINE™ SERIES (3⅛" thick)					
CIRRUS™	x	x			x
DECORA®	x	x		x	x
DELPHI®	x	x		x	x
PREMIERE SERIES					
	SOLAR REFLECTIVE Block (3⅞" thick)				
DECORA® & VUE®		x			
	HEDRON® I Corner Block (Compatible with both series)				
DECORA®	x	x			
	TRIDRON 45° Block® Units (Compatible with both series)				
DECORA® & VUE®		x (8" High)			
	EndBlock™ Finishing Unit (3⅞" thick)				
DECORA®		x			
	EndBlock™ Finishing Unit (3⅛" thick)				
DECORA®					x
	Encurve™ Finishing Unit (3⅞" thick)				
DECORA®		x			
	PAVER Units (DELPHI® Pattern, 1" thick)				
DELPHI®	x (6"x 6" Actual)				

* Metric sizes also are available. Please call Pittsburgh Corning for details.

The Pittsburgh Corning Promise—The comprehensive variety of patterns, styles and sizes available have been designed to work together in your home as a total system. Pittsburgh Corning stands behind all PC GlassBlock® units when used exclusively with other PC GlassBlock® units and accessories by offering a limited five-year warranty.

OTHER OPTIONS

LX FIBROUS GLASS INSERTS:
These versatile inserts add significant light, privacy and thermal control by tempering glare, light transmission and solar heat gain.

SOLAR REFLECTIVE COATING:
The highly reflective, thermally bonded oxide surface coating reduces light transmission up to 95 percent more and solar heat gain up to 80 percent more than conventional ⅛-inch plate glass.

PAVER UNITS:
Designed for horizontal use in stairways and walkways. Solid-glass 1-inch-thick Delphi® pattern.

EDGE COATING:
On special order, the edge coating of glass block can be replaced with black or brown. To further enhance the effect of the edge coating, use coordinated tinted mortars.

PC® GLASS CAPS:
Add decorative appeal to finishing glass block with this new accessory product. PC® Glass caps can be used to finish off applications of both 8"x 8" Regular Series and 8"x 8" Thinline Series. Available in five sizes in both black and white, PC® Glass caps can also be used with PC GlassBlock® HEDRON® I Corner Block and the EndBlock™ Finishing Units.

Installation Methods

Mortar with VeriTru® Spacers

Installing Pittsburgh Corning PC GlassBlock® Products with mortar gives you or your contractor great potential: Curves, multistory expanses, exterior and interior applications, shower enclosures and more are all within possibility. The details at right show you the accessories you'll need to complete the installation with success.

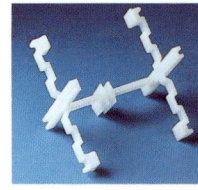

VeriTru® Spacers
One-piece, all-plastic VeriTru® Spacer speeds construction, assures uniform placement and helps keep panels flush.

How to Install Pittsburgh Corning PC GlassBlock® Products Video
Whether you're planning to install glass block yourself or hiring a contractor, you'll see all that is involved — every step of the way — in all three of the installation types in this complete video, How to Install PC GlassBlock® Products. A copy for you is available for purchase at your local Pittsburgh Corning distributor or select homecenters.

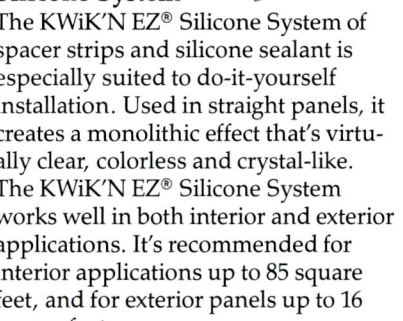

KWiK'N EZ® Silicone System

The KWiK'N EZ® Silicone System of spacer strips and silicone sealant is especially suited to do-it-yourself installation. Used in straight panels, it creates a monolithic effect that's virtually clear, colorless and crystal-like. The KWiK'N EZ® Silicone System works well in both interior and exterior applications. It's recommended for interior applications up to 85 square feet, and for exterior panels up to 16 square feet.

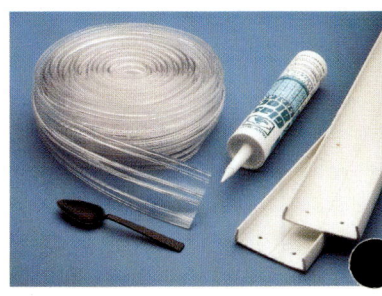

Preassembled Pittsburgh Corning PC GlassBlock® Panels

Here's a labor-saving product that's perfect for replacement or new-window and small-partition applications. Check with your local Pittsburgh Corning distributor for availability of preassembled glass block panels in your area.

For more application ideas or technical information regarding construction and product specifications, call the PC GlassBlock® Products Hotline: 800-992-5769.

FIVE-YEAR LIMITED WARRANTY
Pittsburgh Corning Corporation, ("PC"), promises to replace any glass blocks that are found to be defective within five years from the date of purchase. We will not replace blocks damaged as a result of faulty installation. Upon discovery of any defect, you should send written notice to Pittsburgh Corning Corporation, 800 Presque Isle Drive, Pittsburgh, PA 15239—Attention: PC GlassBlock® Customer Service Department, or telephone 412/327-6100. A proof of purchase and a sample or photograph of the block(s) in question will be required. PC will review your claim and replace any block(s) found to be defective.
  Your sole remedy is replacement of defective blocks, excluding labor, and **PC will not be liable for any incidental or consequential damages relating to your purchase or use of PC Glass Blocks.** All implied warranties are also limited to a duration of five years from the date of your purchase of PC GlassBlock® products. Some states do not allow the exclusion or limitation of incidental or consequential damages, or the limitation on how long an implied warranty lasts, so the above limitations may not apply to you. This warranty gives you specific legal rights and you may also have other rights which vary from state to state.
  The information contained herein is accurate and reliable to the best of our knowledge. But, because Pittsburgh Corning Corporation has no control over installation workmanship, accessory materials or conditions of application, NO EXPRESS OR IMPLIED WARRANTY OF ANY KIND, INCLUDING THOSE OF MERCHANTABILITY OR FITNESS FOR A PARTICULAR PURPOSE, IS MADE as to the performance of an installation containing Pittsburgh Corning products. In no event shall Pittsburgh Corning be liable for any damages arising because of product failure, whether incidental, special, consequential or punitive, regardless of the theory of liability upon which any such damages are claimed. Pittsburgh Corning Corporation provides written warranties for many of its products, and such warranties take precedence over the statements contained herein.
Warranty is valid in Canada.

ISO 9003 Certification

PC®, PC GlassBlock®, ARGUS®, DECORA®, DELPHI®, ESSEX®, HEDRON®, KWiK'N EZ®, TRIDRON 45° Block®, VeriTru®, VISTABRIK® and VUE® are federally registered trademarks, and CIRRUS™, Encurve™, EndBlock™, THINLINE™ and TEXTRA™ are trademarks, owned by Pittsburgh Corning Corporation.

© 1994, 1995 Pittsburgh Corning Corporation

PITTSBURGH CORNING

Pittsburgh Corning Corporation
800 Presque Isle Drive
Pittsburgh, PA 15239
Tel: (412) 327-6100

PC GlassBlock® Products Information Hotline 800-992-5769
(Continental U.S./Canada, Weekdays 8-5:00 ET)

SOLAR
white

Structurally engineered preglazed hollow glass block and aluminum assemblies are offered for installation as sky lights, barrel vaults, sky bridges, floor and deck lights, wall panels and complete structures. See our descriptive brochure in SWEETS section 07810/CIR.

SolarWhite Glass Block and Aluminum Skylight, Floor & Deck Light, and Wall Panels™

Front Cover
Left Photo:
91R Steel Panels, Capital Bank Miami, Florida.
Architects: Gensler & Associates/Architects, New York & Houston.
Photography: Nick Merrick Hedrich Blessing, Chicago, Illinois.

Top Photo:
Solar White Aluminum Panels, Woodbridge, Connecticut Residence.
Architect: Kagan Architects and Planners, Gerald M. Kagan, AIA Principal, New Haven, Connecticut.
General Contractor: The Panza Construction Company, West Haven, Connecticut.
Photography: Sunny Clarke.

Bottom Photo:
71R Concrete Panels, Metro West Clubhouse, Orlando, Florida.
Architects: The Evans Group, Orlando, Florida.
General Contractor: Lecesse Corporation, Orlando, Florida.
Photography: Sunny Clarke.

04270/CIR
Buyline 5914

Connecticut Residence, Porch Over Swimming Pool. Architect: Thompson & Scarlett, Southfield, Massachusetts. General Contractor: Palmer Building Company, Winsted, Connecticut.

Standard and custom sizes and a variety of glass block designs are available. Glass block panels for various applications including floor and deck lights, stair treads and landings, sidewalks and sky bridges are also available in steel and concrete systems preglazed with solid paver glass blocks.

Glass Block and Concrete Floor and Deck Light Panels™

71R

Rivercenter Mall and Water Feature San Antonio, Texas. Owner: the Edward J. DeBartolo Corporation, Youngstown, Ohio. Architect: Urban Design Group, Tulsa, Oklahoma. General Contractor: Manhattan Construction Company, Dallas, Texas. Fountain Designer: William Hobbs, Ltd., Atlanta, Georgia. Photography: Sunny Clarke.

04270/CIR
Buyline 5914

Structurally engineered preglazed solid glass block and concrete assemblies are offered for installation as floor and deck lights, stair treads and landings, sidewalk panels, sky lights and skybridges. Standard and custom surface finishes of concrete, wood, terrazzo and others allow for use in any area. See our descriptive brochure in SWEETS section 03400/CIR. Glass block panels for various horizontal and vertical applications are also available in steel and aluminum systems with a variety of glass block designs.

91R

91R Glass Block and Steel Floor and Deck Light Panels™

Structurally engineered preglazed solid glass block and steel assemblies are offered for installation as floor and deck lights, stair treads and landings, sky lights, and sky bridges using several sizes and styles of solid glass pavers.

04270/CIR
Buyline 5914

Glass block panels for various horizontal and vertical applications are also available in concrete systems with standard and custom finishes of concrete, wood, terrazzo and others as well as hollow glass block and aluminum systems with a variety of glass block designs for use in any area.

91R Steel Panels, Corning Incorporated Headquarters, Corning, New York. Architects: Kevin Roche John Dinkeloo and Associates, Hamden, Connecticut. General Contractor: Morganti Inc., Danbury, Connecticut. Photography: Ron Meadows, Meadows Marketing, Inc.

04270/CIR
Buyline 5914

CIRCLE REDMONT, INC.
1-800-358-3888

71R Concrete Floor Panels, Chicago Historical Society, Chicago, Illinois.
Architects: Holabird & Root, Chicago, Illinois.
General Contractor: Pepper Construction Co., Chicago, Illinois.
Photography: Sunny Clarke.

Circle Redmont offers prefabricated glass block panels for installation as skylights, barrel vaults, skybridges, floor and deck lights, stairtreads and landings, sidewalks, wall panels and complete structures. Structurally engineered, preglazed and fully waterproof, these panels are available in many standard and custom sizes and a variety of glass block designs.

No other manufacturer or on-site fabrication method can give you this package of Circle Redmont advantages:

- Easy installation, usually as simple as lift and lay.
- Replaceable glass blocks, if ever necessary, without damaging the surrounding structure.
- All panels engineered for specific job requirements (e.g. loading, surrounding structure, thermodynamics).
- Decades of experience with thousand of successful applications worldwide.
- Proprietary setting materials and sealants which we have developed specifically to:
  - compensate for thermodynamic forces (temperature, wind, expansion/contraction) without damaging the glass blocks.
  - provide proper seal between dissimilar materials.
  - ensure the structural integrity and loadbearing capacity of the composite structure.

Call Circle Redmont for design assistance, engineering, fabrication and warranty of all our custom and standard systems.

CIRCLE REDMONT

GLASS BLOCK PANELS

CIRCLE REDMONT, INC.
1-800-358-3888 2760 BUSINESS CENTER, BLVD. MELBOURNE FL 32940 407-259-7374 FAX 407-259-7237

B667
04270/GLA
BuyLine 6786

GLASS BLOCK

- 50 PATTERNS
- 21 SIZES
- 7 COLORS

PRINTED IN USA

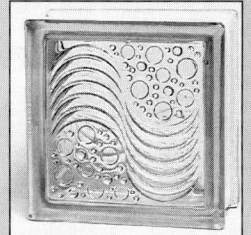
BONZAI

DUO

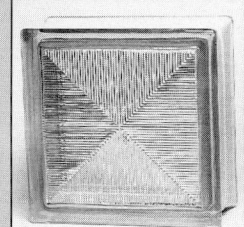
QUATRO

STARBURST

RIPPLE

ANDROMEDA

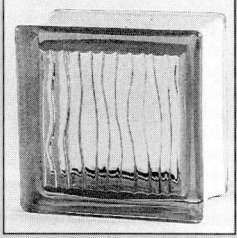
GHOST

RIBBED (BROAD)

BULLET RESISTANT

SILK

COSMOS

NAUTILUS

RIBBED (NARROW)

NEPTUNE

CRYSTAL (ALSO IN CORNER & BULLNOSE)

BUBBLE

VENUS

WAVE

WAVE BULLNOSE (ALSO IN CLEAR)

WAVE CORNER (ALSO IN CLEAR)

PRODUCT LINE UP

PRODUCT LINE UP	WIDTH 3-1/8"									WIDTH 3-7/8"						TECHNICAL							
	4-1/2 X 4-1/2	4-1/2 X 9-1/2	4 X 8	6 X 6	6 X 8	7-3/4 X 7-3/4	8 X 8	10 X 10	12 X 12	4 X 8	6 X 6	6 X 12	7-3/4 X 7-3/4	8 X 8	10 X 10	12 X 12	THERMAL EXPANSION COEFFICIENT	SOUND LOSS ACCOUSTIC INSULATION, dB	COMPRESSIVE STRENGTH PSI	IMPACT STRENGTH LBS/INCH	U VALUE HEAT TRANSMISSION	R VALUE THERMAL TRANSMISSION	LIGHT TRANSMISSION	SHADING COEFFICIENT
WEIGHT LBS	2.2	3.9	2.9	3.1	4.5	4.8	5.3	7.7	13.7	3.6	3.5	7.6	6	6.4	9.7	15.3								
BONZAI						●					●			●			47 X 10⁻⁷	42	800-1000	50-55	48-53	2.08	80%	.65
VENUS						●					●			●			47 X 10⁻⁷	42	800-1000	50-55	48-53	2.08	80%	.65
CRYSTAL	ALSO IN CORNER & BULLNOSE										●	●		●			47 X 10⁻⁷	42	800-1000	50-55	48-53	2.08	80%	.65
DUO																●	47 X 10⁻⁷	42	800-1000	50-55	48-53	2.08	80%	.65
GHOST							●							●			47 X 10⁻⁷	42	800-1000	50-55	48-53	2.08	80%	.65
NAUTILUS						●								●	●		47 X 10⁻⁷	42	800-1000	50-55	48-53	2.08	80%	.65
QUATRO						●								●			47 X 10⁻⁷	42	800-1000	50-55	48-53	2.08	80%	.65
RIBBED BROAD	●	●		●		●	●	●	●		●		●	●		●	47 X 10⁻⁷	42	800-1000	50-55	48-53	2.08	80%	.65
RIBBED NARROW	●	●		●		●	●	●	●		●		●	●		●	47 X 10⁻⁷	42	800-1000	50-55	48-53	2.08	80%	.65
SILK														●			47 X 10⁻⁷	42	800-1000	50-55	48-53	2.08	80%	.65
STARBURST						●								●			47 X 10⁻⁷	42	800-1000	50-55	48-53	2.08	80%	.65
WAVE	●	●	●	●	●	●	●			●	●		●	●			47 X 10⁻⁷	42	800-1000	50-55	48-53	2.08	80%	.65
WAVE BULLNOSE	ALSO IN CRYSTAL			●	●	OR CLEAR					●	●					47 X 10⁻⁷	42	800-1000	50-55	48-53	2.08	80%	.65
WAVE CORNER	ALSO IN CRYSTAL			●	●	OR CLEAR					●	●					47 X 10⁻⁷	42	800-1000	50-55	48-53	2.08	80%	.65
BULLET RESISTANT	ALSO IN CLEAR PATTERN										●			●			47 X 10⁻⁷	48	3050	120	30	3.23	80%	.65
BUBBLE			●		●	●	●							●			47 X 10⁻⁷	42	800-1000	50-55	48-53	2.08	80%	.65
COSMOS			●			●											47 X 10⁻⁷	42	800-1000	50-55	48-53	2.08	80%	.65
RIPPLE						●								●			47 X 10⁻⁷	42	800-1000	50-55	48-53	2.08	80%	.65
NEPTUNE						●		●									47 X 10⁻⁷	42	800-1000	50-55	48-53	2.08	80%	.65
ANDROMEDA			●	●	●	●											47 X 10⁻⁷	42	800-1000	50-55	48-53	2.08	80%	.65
DARK BLUE						●	●	●									47 X 10⁻⁷	42	800-1000	50-55	48-53	2.08	62%	.42
LIGHT BLUE						●	●	●									47 X 10⁻⁷	42	800-1000	50-55	48-53	2.08	62%	.42
BRONZE						●	●	●									47 X 10⁻⁷	42	800-1000	50-55	48-53	2.08	62%	.42
GREEN						●	●	●									47 X 10⁻⁷	42	800-1000	50-55	48-53	2.08	62%	.42
GREY						●	●	●									47 X 10⁻⁷	42	800-1000	50-55	48-53	2.08	62%	.42
ROSE						●	●	●									47 X 10⁻⁷	42	800-1000	50-55	48-53	2.08	62%	.42
OPALINE	ALSO IN FLAT FINISH										●	●					47 X 10⁻⁷	42	800-1000	50-55	48-53	2.08	62%	.42

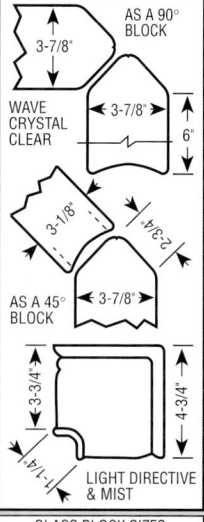

CORNER DETAILS

AS A 90° BLOCK
3-7/8"
WAVE CRYSTAL CLEAR
3-7/8"
6"

3-1/8"
2-3/4"

AS A 45° BLOCK
3-7/8"

3-3/4"
4-3/4"
1-1/4"

LIGHT DIRECTIVE & MIST

GLASS BLOCK SIZES

NOMINAL	ACTUAL
3-1/8"	80MM
3-7/8"	97MM
4"	110MM
4-1/2"	115MM
6"	145MM
7-3/4"	190MM
8"	197MM
9-1/2"	240MM
12"	300MM

BARK

LENS (A HOLLOW BLOCK)

POINT

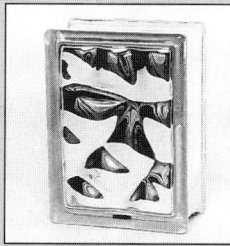
SOLAR REFLECTIVE (WAVE)

CLEAR (ALSO IN CORNER & BULLNOSE)

CORONA

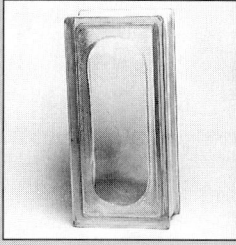
LOOP (6" X 12")

MOSAIC

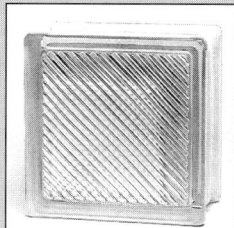
CUT

VASES/PIGGY BANK

MIST CORNERS

MIST

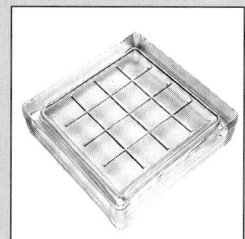
PRISM PAVERS

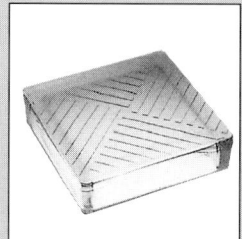
NON-SLIP PAVERS

WINDOW (GALVANIZED POWDERCOAT)

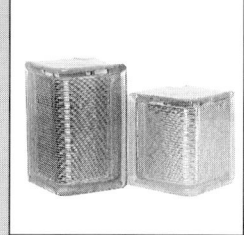
LIGHT DIRECTIVE CNR

LIGHT DIRECTIVE (LD)

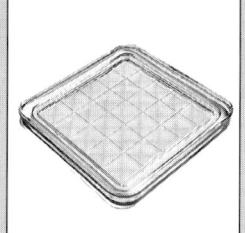
SOLID PAVERS

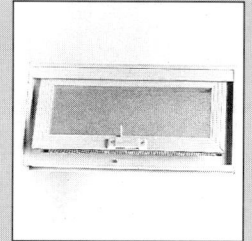
WINDOWS (VINYL)

ACCESSORIES

PRODUCT LINE UP

	WIDTH 3-1/8"									WIDTH 3-7/8"						PAVERS				TECHNICAL							
	4-1/2 X 4-1/2	4-1/2 X 9-1/2	4 X 8	6 X 6	6 X 8	7-3/4 X 7-3/4	8 X 8	10 X 10	12 X 12	4 X 8	6 X 6	6 X 12	7-3/4 X 7-3/4	8 X 8	10 X 10	12 X 12	120 X 120 X 40MM	160 X 160 X 30MM	200 X 200 X 50MM	200 X 200 X 22MM	THERMAL EXPANSION COEFICIENT	SOUND LOSS ACCOUSTIC INSULATION, dB	COMPRESSIVE STRENGTH PSI	IMPACT STRENGTH LBS/INCH	U VALUE HEAT TRANSMISSION	R VALUE THERMAL TRANSMISSION	LIGHT TRANSMISSION	SHADING COEFFICIENT
WEIGHT LBS	2.2	3.9	2.9	3.1	4.5	4.8	5.3	7.7	13.7	3.6	3.5	7.6	6	6.4	9.7	15.3												
BARK											●										47×10^{-7}	42	800-1000	50-55	48-53	2.08	80%	.65
CORONA											●	●	●								47×10^{-7}	42	800-1000	50-55	48-53	2.08	80%	.65
CLEAR	●	●	●	●	●	●	●	●	●	●	●		●	●		●					47×10^{-7}	42	800-1000	50-55	48-53	2.08	80%	.65
CUT											●		●								47×10^{-7}	42	800-1000	50-55	48-53	2.08	80%	.65
LENS	140MM DIA X 95MM																				47×10^{-7}	42	800-1000	50-55	48-53	2.08	80%	.65
LOOP												●									47×10^{-7}	42	800-1000	50-55	48-53	2.08	80%	.65
LIGHT DIRECTIVE						●					●		●		●						47×10^{-7}	42	800-1000	50-55	48-53	2.08	80%	.65
LD CORNERS 90°											●		●								47×10^{-7}	42	800-1000	50-55	48-53	2.08	80%	.65
NON-SLIP PAVERS																	●		●		47×10^{-7}	42	800-1000	50-55	48-53	2.08	80%	.49
PRISM PAVERS																	●	●			47×10^{-7}	42	800-1000	50-55	48-53	2.08	80%	.65
SOLID PAVERS																				●	47×10^{-7}	42	800-1000	50-55	48-53	2.08	80%	.65
POINT	●																				47×10^{-7}	42	800-1000	50-55	48-53	2.08	80%	.65
SOLAR REF RIBBED*											●										47×10^{-7}	42	800-1000	50-55	48-53	2.08	15%	.25
SOLAR REF CLEAR*	●	●									●		●		●						47×10^{-7}	42	800-1000	50-55	48-53	2.08	15%	.25
SOLAR REF WAVE	●										●		●								47×10^{-7}	42	800-1000	50-55	48-53	2.08	15%	.25
MIST	●	●			●		●				●		●								47×10^{-7}	42	800-1000	50-55	48-53	2.08	80%	.65
MIST CORNERS 90°											●		●								47×10^{-7}	42	800-1000	50-55	48-53	2.08	80%	.65
MIST WAVE *											●	●									47×10^{-7}	42	800-1000	50-55	48-53	2.08	80%	.65
MOSAIC			●			●	●														47×10^{-7}	42	800-1000	50-55	48-53	2.08	80%	.65
VASES	AVAILABLE IN 10" X 10", 5" X 10", 4" X 8", 8" X 8". 6" X 6" & 4" X 4" – IN BUBBLE & WAVE																											
WINDOWS/VINYL	RIGID WHITE VINYL AVAILABLE FROM 6" X 6" TO 32" X 32"																											
WINDOW/GALVANIZED	ELECTRO GALVANIZED STEEL POWDER COATED, 8" X 8"																											
ACCESSORIES	EXPANSION STRIP, JOINT REINFORCING, SPACERS, WALL ANCHOR – SPECIFICATION & INSTALLATION MANUAL AVAILABLE																											
SURFACE FROSTING	ALUMINUM OXIDE SURFACE FROSTING AVAILABLE ON ALL BLOCK																											
COLORED EDGE	COLORED RIMS AVAILABLE ON ALL BLOCK, 8 COLORS																											
END CAP TILE	AVAILABLE IN 12 COLORS: SAGE, TAUPE, SMOKE, GREY, BLACK, WHITE, ROSE, DUSTY ROSE, WINE, COPPER GREEN, ICE BLUE & NAVY																											

*THIS BLOCK IS NOT SHOWN

AZUR CLOUD
GERMANY
7.5"X7.5"X3.125"

AZUR MATT
GERMANY
7.5"X7.5"X3.125"

BLUE CLOUD
GERMANY
7.5"X7.5"X3.125"

BLUE MATT
GERMANY
7.5"X7.5"X3.125"

CLEAR MATT
GERMANY
7.5"X7.5"X3.125"

TURKIS CLOUD
GERMANY
7.5"X7.5"X3.125"

TURKIS MATT
GERMANY
7.5"X7.5"X3.125"

GREEN CLOUD
GERMANY
7.5"X7.5"X3.125"

ROSE CLOUD
GERMANY
7.5"X7.5"X3.125"

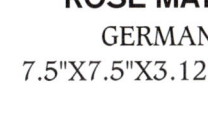

ROSE MATT
GERMANY
7.5"X7.5"X3.125"

GREY CLOUD
GERMANY
7.5"X7.5"X3.125"

BRONZE CLOUD
GERMANY
7.5"X7.5"X3.125"

GREY MATT
GERMANY
7.5"X7.5"X3.125"

CLEAR
GERMANY
6"X6"X4"
8"x8"x4"
12"x12"x4"
4"x8"x4"
6"x6"x3.125"
8"x8"x3.125"
4"x8"x3.125"

CROSS-RIBBED
GERMANY
6"X6"X4"
8"X8"X4"
12"X12"X4"

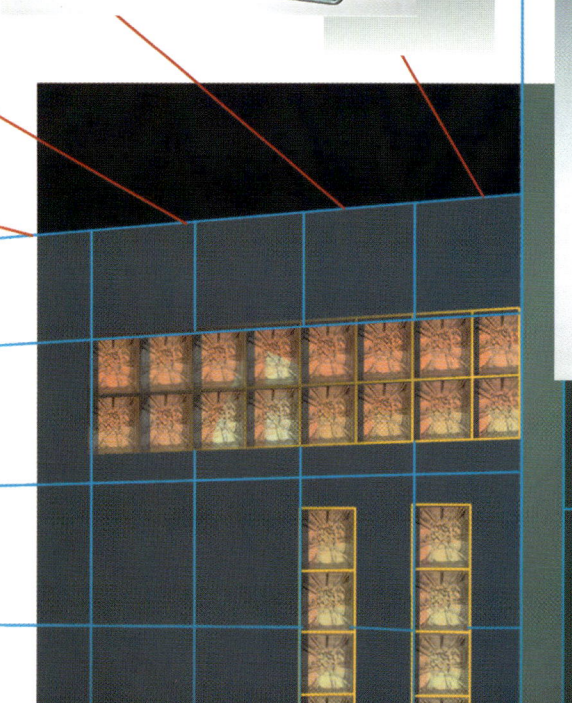

CLOUD
GERMANY
6"X6"X4"
8"x8"x4"
12"x12"x4"
4"x8"x4"
6"x6"x3.125"
8"x8"x3.125"
4"x8"x3.125"

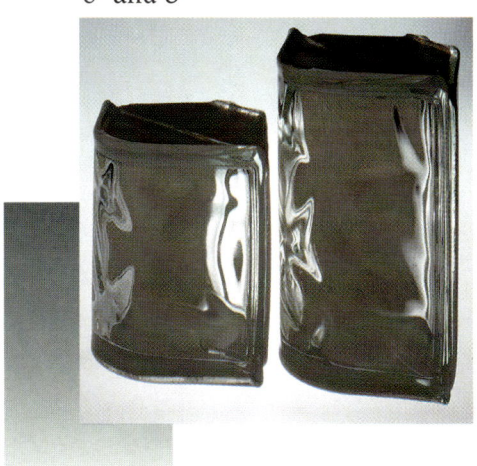

CORNER
GERMANY
6" and 8"

END BLOCK
GERMANY
8"X8"X4"

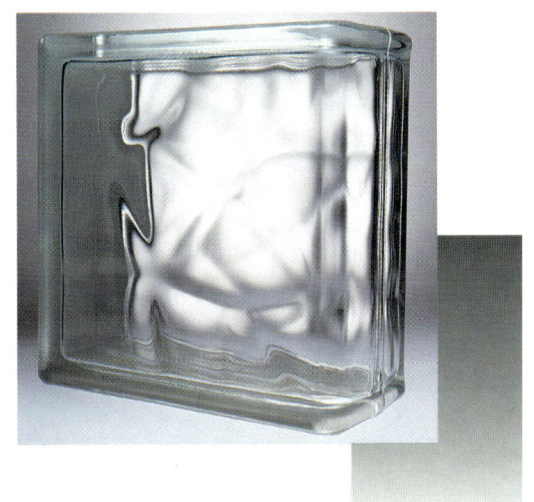

DOUBLE END
GERMANY
8"X8"X4"

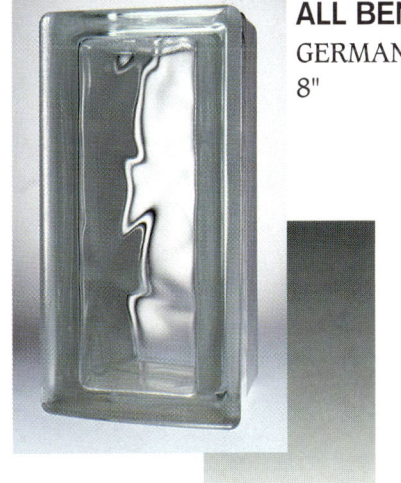

ALL BEND
GERMANY
8"

LR
GERMANY
7.5"X7.5"X3.125"

GEMEX
GERMANY
6"X6"X3"
8"x8"x3"

SAVONA
GERMANY
7.5"X7.5"X3.125"

STELLA (Matt)
GERMANY
7.5"X7.5"X3.125"

COLLIER
GERMANY
7.5"X7.5"X3.125"

DIGONA
GERMANY
7.5"X7.5"X3.125"

MOSAIC
GERMANY
7.5"X7.5"X3.125"

MALTA
GERMANY
7.5"X7 .5"X3.125"

REFLEX
GERMANY
7.5"X7.5"X3.125"

KOSMOS
GERMANY
7.5"X7.5"X3.125"

DIADEM
GERMANY
7.5"X7.5"X3.125"

ALPHA
GERMANY
9.5"X9.5"X3.125"

WOGE
GERMANY
9.5"X9.5"X3.125"

ACHAT
GERMANY
9.5"X9.5"X3.125"

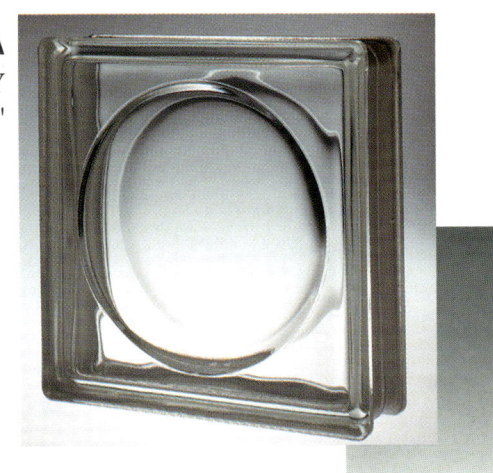

DIAMANT
GERMANY
9.5"X9.5"X3.125"

KARAT
GERMANY
9.5"X9.5"X3.125"

JUPITER
GERMANY
9.5"X9.5"X3.125"

ORION
GERMANY
9.5"X9.5"X3.125"

STAR
GERMANY
9.5"X9.5"X3.125"

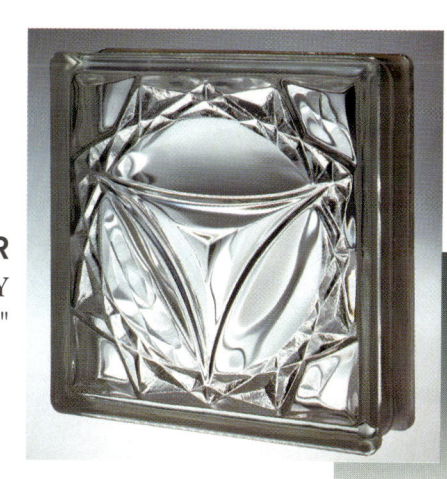

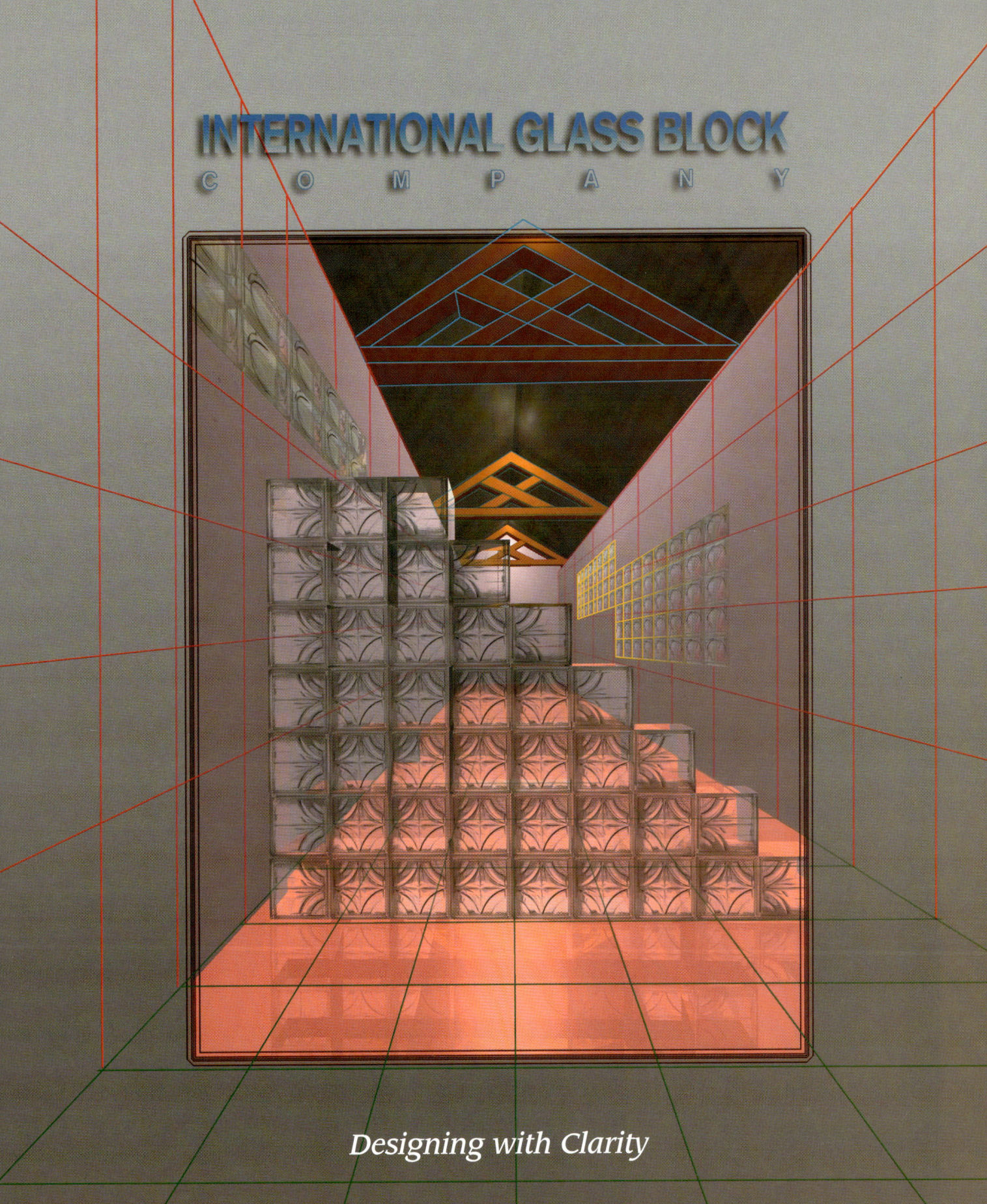